Kick Start Your Online Marketing in 21 Days!

Every day for 21 days, I will email you a quick & easy task to

do that will get your online marketing humming...

Think of it as positive reinforcement of what you have learnt in this book. Each task has a short video showing you what you need to do and how to do it.

- Simple to do
- Once a day
- Gets things moving
- Guaranteed to work

As a free gift to you for reading my book, I'd like to give this course to you. It's free to sign up now! All you need to do is go to the web page below and start:

http://21days.mrwebmarketing.com

FREE GIFT!

7 Steps to Getting More Business Online in Less Time!

The Billion Dollar Blueprint

7 Steps To Getting More Business Online in Less Time!

Brad Hauck

The Billion Dollar Blueprint: 7 Steps To Getting More Business Online in Less Time!

© 2013 Brad Hauck

Australian Institute of Online Marketing Pty Ltd

ACN: 141 706 130

Foreword

To say that Brad Hauck knows how to get business on the Internet is a huge understatement. Brad is commonly known as Mr Web Marketing; he is the undisputed master of online marketing and more than 50 million people can testify to the fact. That's the number of visitors Brad has bought to clients and his own websites over the past five years.

Working on the premise that for many businesses, their website is 'the laziest member of staff', Brad takes the internet marketing black box, gets rid of the hype, distils the essence of what works and uses that information to help businesses get results.

Brad knows how a combination of quality training, a well-defined plan of action and the implementation of a range of internet marketing techniques can readily achieve better rankings, increased traffic, improved conversions and ultimately, more business from web marketing. Working alongside small and large businesses, Brad has achieved astounding results helping clients achieve millions of dollars worth of sales online.

Brad initially trained as a telecommunications technician before becoming a teacher. He has a Dip Teaching and a Masters in Education. In 1996 he found his niche in online marketing and has spent the past 16 years honing his skills. As CEO of the Australian Institute of Internet Marketing, Brad trains people to succeed online.

When not fuelling his passion for fantastic online marketing results, Brad spends time fighting fires in his capacity as a Volunteer Rural Fire Officer.

As the 2013 President of the National Speakers Association of Australia's Qld Chapter, Brad speaks at conferences and events all over the world about getting more people to your website and driving online sales. His topics include:

- The Billion Dollar Blueprint
- Avoiding Social Media Disasters
- Increasing Productivity Online for Massive Results
- Living the 4 Hour Work Week
- Online Reputation Management
- Other custom topics by request.

You can book Brad today for your next conference, event or seminar by calling **1300 793 700** or by going to:

- www.mrwebmarketing.com.au

- www.aiimtraining.com.au

This book is dedicated to:

My family whom I love and who constantly surprise me with their unwavering support despite having to live with my "Idea of the Day" mind.

My mentors without whom I would drift uselessly in the wind with no focus at all.

My mates in the Rural Fire Service. We fight fires, protect our community and will literally walk over hot coals to help each other.

Introduction

Hype, Jargon & Black boxes

Introduction: Hype, Jargon & Black Boxes

The internet is awash with gurus, experts and masters of hype, jargon and black boxes spouting about the "next big thing" all apparently guaranteed to make you millions in minutes.

I'm not going to do that.

Why? Because I'd be lying to you if I did. Success online requires "elbow grease", a plan and focus.

Besides, it's just not my style. My style is about teaching you how to get massive results faster in less time each day based on the techniques and skills that have worked consistently and safely for over 10 years.

My main goal here is to help you succeed online.

Since 1996, I've applied or taught the 7 steps you're about to learn, over and over to help thousands of businesses get better rankings, increase conversions and results online.

Some of these websites were my own but many belonged to others selling anything from car servicing to million dollar apartments and everything in between.

During that time, I have spoken to audiences all over Australia and New Zealand helping them to get a handle on their online marketing without the confusing "techie speak".

The Challenge

The fact is that no matter what it is that you're trying to sell online from paperclips to appointments, and how much you already know about online marketing, I would bet that you're not following my steps on an ongoing basis.

Most businesses will not consistently go past Step 2 although they may dabble in Steps 3-6 once or twice.

I challenge you to apply all 7 Steps for 6 months! 12 months would be better still.

If you can implement these steps and continue to apply them, I can guarantee that you'll see a huge change in your results. I've seen websites go from 10 visitors a day to 500 a day in just 3 months by applying these steps.

Why is Marketing Your Business Online Important?

Given that you're reading this book, I'm probably preaching to the converted but no business can go without some sort of web presence these days.

I know of people who have not phoned a business just because they don't have a website. From another angle, in many businesses it's the junior office person who gets the job of searching for new suppliers and contractors and they just about always start that search online.

I was amazed to discover from interviewing people that they often don't go past Google when searching and if they don't like the look of your website, they won't ring you... even if you're the best at what you do!

You Don't Know What You Don't Know

If you're not leveraging the internet for your business, you don't know what you are missing out on.

It might not lead to a hundred new sales every day but wouldn't even 10 leads a day make a massive difference over 12 months? That's roughly 3640 more leads a year!

Many of the people I speak to who haven't launched onto the Internet in a focused way, have not done so because they're unsure where to start and what they should do first. By the time you get to the end of my 7 steps, this won't be a problem for you.

You'll understand what you need to do and what the first step is once you have your website.

If you find that you need a hand, I do consult and help

businesses get their marketing moving. You can find me at **www.mrwebmarketing.com**.

So why is this book called "The Billion Dollar Blueprint"?

A recent online shopping Report forecasts that online sales in Australia will grow from $27 billion in 2010 to an expected $37.1 billion in 2013 *(eCommerce Report.com.au)*

That's retail. It doesn't even take into consideration service providers, such as all of the plumbers, the lawyers, and other service businesses. It doesn't take into account how much money they're making from their websites or how many sales they're making via the phone from online advertising.

These figures just continue to grow and evolve. This is what could be a very small $ amount compared to the truth. **I personally feel it is probably about a $100 Billion** or more because there are so many hidden business transactions that wouldn't be counted in that report. There's also a lot of small & micro businesses selling online who might not get counted.

Did you know that retail spending via the internet grew approximately 26% to hit $12.3 billion in the year ending October 2012? *(NAB Retail Sales Index, 2012)* This is supported by a report by the Australian Communications and Media Authority (ACMA) who indicate that online shopping activities grew 27% in the 12 months to July 12, 2012.

Sadly, 66 per cent of retailers believe that international online retailers have impacted their sales. Of this group, 37% believe they have had a large or very large impact. *(Experian, Oct 2012)*.

From my point of view, the best part is that only 1/3 of the top retail websites being used by Australians are based outside Australia. This tells me that some Australian businesses are seizing the opportunity with both hands and running with it.

Are you?

Let's Get Started

I guess it's time that I let you get started on your journey. So sit back, sharpen your virtual pencil and get ready to take some notes as you work your way through these 7 essential steps to getting more business online faster!

Have fun!

Brad Hauck ☺

Step 1

Learn What The Search Engines Want And Do It.

Step 1: Learn What the Search Engines Want and Do It

Let's face it, even with all the hype around new technology, the search engines are normally the first place you'd start looking for things – products, services, and information.

No matter which way you look at it, it's <u>essential</u> for your business to be found in Google and the other search engines like Bing and Yahoo for what you do or sell.

This is where your market it, this is where everyone will look for you and where you **need** to be found.

A recent PayPal & eBay report shows that 95% of online Australians now use online media for their research. These actions often lead to an in-store (75%)or an online purchase (71%).

Very few, 5%, have <u>never</u> gone on to make a purchase. *(Sensis® Social Media Report)*

What's It Worth?

Getting into the top 3 on Google is worth a lot of money to a business. If you didn't know, roughly 56% of the clicks go to the person in the #1 spot, followed by 13% for #2 and 9% for #3 . It falls away quickly after that.

Have a look at the image on the next page. It was taken in 2006 from an eye tracking study of people using Google when searching for information. Based upon many conversations I've had over the years, it still holds true to a large extent today although 2nd & 3rd may be closer to 20% now.

	% of Clicks	% Time Spent
	56.36	28.43
	13.45	25.08
	9.82	14.72
	4.00	8.70
	4.73	6.02
	3.27	4.01
	0.36	3.01
	2.91	3.68
	1.45	3.01
	2.55	2.34

http://www.seoresearcher.com/distribution-of-clicks-on-googles-serps-and-eye-tracking-analysis.htm

If those percentages aren't enough to prove to you why you need to get high rankings in the search engines, I don't know what is!

Think about it... if you're in position #1 you get 56 of every 100 visitors. If 1 out of 5 buy a $100 product or service from you, you make $1100 in extra sales a day. That's $400,400 a year in your bank account!

Now compare that with position #2 – 13/100. Working on the same figures, you make an extra $200 a day or $72800 a year.

That's a loss of over $300,000 in sales. I can't imagine anybody who would knowingly pass up that much money. Would you?

If you don't take high search rankings seriously, you are missing the cream of the clients that you could be capturing. In today's marketplace, that cream will be going to your competitors and an extra $300K a year is going to put them in a much more powerful advertising position to you!

Know this, if you're at #6 on page 1 of Google, you really don't know how many leads you're missing because what you see in your analytics is no real indicator of the potential traffic. It's a logarithmic increase.

So What Do The Search Engines Want?

Google has always made it very clear about what they're trying to do and what they want from websites who are aiming for higher rankings.

Google wants to provide the best possible answer to a user's search as quickly and efficiently as possible. Localised search is also playing an increasingly more important role as they try to supply results based on the user's local area e.g. results in Sydney only.

If you want better rankings, you need to provide quality information that the search engines can index, and also help them to index it correctly.

You need to look at what you need to do to make it work for you. Even though it seems like there's a lot of changes happening in search ranking algorithms, the essential skills and techniques have remained basically the same. This hasn't changed since I first started selling online in about '96.

What clouds the facts is that you get a lot of hype on the web. There's always something new. There's always something cool. There's always something better that you should be doing on the web.

But, when it comes down to brass tacks, you'll find that if you get the Search engine optimization (SEO) right on your website, you can actually pickup most of the traffic you want.

It is important to note though that some industries are over competitive. This doesn't mean that you can't get great traffic through SEO, it means that you have to choose a tight niche to work in.

Most businesses do not complete the SEO process so they tend to feel that it's a waste of time and money. The companies that have realised that it's important own the top spots and the traffic. It's well worth your time to do ensure that you learn SEO.

How Do You Get Those Rankings?

You need to optimise your website.

Commonly known as Search Engine Optimisation (SEO), it's basically a process that makes your website more search engine friendly. You do this by ensuring that it meets the guidelines that the search engines say they want to see, and you throw in a little "magic" or "art".

That's why it's sometimes called the "Art of Search Engine Optimisation". You discover the small changes needed through ongoing testing.

According to Wikipedia, "SEO is the process of improving the visibility of a website or a web page in search engines via the "natural" or un-paid ("organic" or "algorithmic") search results."

It doesn't take much effort to discover how to do basic SEO and you can learn the introductory skills in a matter of hours. The problem is that hardly any businesses get around to applying those skills to their website.

The main thing you need to understand is that, with SEO, there are multiple ways of getting listings on the front-page. There's not just the pages from your own website. There are sites like Facebook Pages, Twitter, Google+ Profiles, videos, and other authority sites like Squidoo to name a few.

All these sites will get you organic results and put your business on the first page of Google. If you do it right, you can control the listings for the first ten spots.

It's extremely hard to do because obviously you're competing against other businesses who are doing the same thing but if you can do it, it's worth it. You can certainly hold the top 10 places for your own business name.

Imagine if no matter what keywords a person looked for (related to your product or service) their only choice was you... Would that make a difference to your bottom line?

To get better results from optimization, you need to get an understanding of the search engines and how they think and display your business.

What are the parts of a search engine result?

This example is for JWA Business & Wealth who are accountants based on the Gold Coast. You'll see there are three text components. You've got the blue text (or purple once visited), you've got the black text and you've got the green text.

Gold Coast Accountants - **Joe Walsh & Associates** Business ...
www.jwa.com.au/

by Joe Walsh
As Gold Coast Business Accountants concentrating on business tax, we work
with business owners and directors in the areas of Financial Management, ...

The blue text is the title of your webpage.

Gold Coast Accountant for Businesses – Joe Walsh & Associates...

The black is content from the webpage that Google chooses or information from the description meta tag.

> As Gold Coast Business Accountants concentrating on business tax we work with business owners and directors in the areas of Financial Management...

The green is the actual link to the website.

> www.jwa.com.au/

It is very important that you understand what the three parts are because everything you now do and write relates to what people see when they do a search. When you write a title, you're writing the blue text.

When you write a description, you're writing the black text. You can't necessarily change your URL but you can give your pages keyword names e.g. tax-planning.html. By doing this, you up your SEO a little bit by showing the search engines that all aspects of the page are about the same topic.

If you're buying a new domain, having a catchy domain name can also encourage people to click on your listing.

Steps for Optimisation

I refer a lot to Google mainly because they own 70% to 80% of current search traffic. Let's face it, Google has become a verb. It's no longer just a place. It's something we just do. If we can concentrate on getting Google right getting Bing and the others isn't so difficult.

In most cases when we look at traffic we find that probably only 7% will come from Bing. It's a very tiny amount but it is growing. Some studies are now showing that Bing is getting almost 30% of all search traffic but that doesn't mean it's going to flow to you in that amount.

In a nutshell, the basic optimisation steps are:

Complete Keyword & niche research

Using a range of tools available for free online, find out what words people are using the most to find your product or service.

- Define the market you're trying to sell to so that you can narrow down your keywords.
- Don't try to be everything to everyone.
- Define your major keyword phrases.
- Pick 3 main keyword phrases that you want to focus on for each website.
- Other related keywords can be added as your optimisation starts to work.

Write and insert a unique Title into every page on your website.

- The title of your page is the words that show up in the very top of your browser window. It is also the first line of the search results.
- Each page on your website must have a unique title which contains the keyword phrases that you are focusing on within that page.

Write and insert a unique Meta Description on every page.

The search engines often use the Meta Description as the second part of the search result listing. Writing keyword-loaded descriptions is a really good opportunity to tell the search engines what you want to display there.

- Each page has to have a unique description that reflects the site and page content.

Ensure that you use your main keywords in page headlines and a couple of times through your content.

It makes sense that on each page you use your main keyword throughout the headlines, headings and text. It's a bit hard to talk about something if you don't mention its name.

- Keep the number of repetitions down to about 4-5 overall. Ignore keyword density and go for human readability.

- Revise your content so that it's focused on 1 keyword per page which matches the one you used in your title, description and headlines.

- Just check over your content to ensure that you have continuity of keyword focus throughout your page. You don't want to be giving the search engines mixed messages.

Name your images.

- If you have a few spare minutes, take the time to fill out a short, keyword-using description of each image on your page.

- Do this by filling in the ALT or alternative description tag. This tag is used by search engines to identify what the image is.

After completing your keyword and niche research, making a small website search engine friendly often only takes a matter of hours. Onsite SEO, as it's known, is the simplest part of the SEO process.

That said, there are good and bad ways of writing titles,

descriptions and headlines. This is the "test and adjust" part of the process.

The hard work comes in when you begin link building back to your site.

Major Pitfalls to Avoid

When I ask most people which words that they would like to rank highly for, they have a habit of handing me a list of hundreds of unrelated keywords. For example a café might choose words like coffee, cake and biscuits.

Obviously these are things they sell but unless they're a wholesale supplier of coffee, cake or biscuits, online they'd be promoting themselves in the wrong area.

A café should be promoted using keywords like coffee shop and café combined with its geographic area – Mudgeeraba, Brisbane or Pacific Fair.

Why? Because most people who are likely to be looking for a café online are probably looking for one locally or near a specific place to meet friends for a drink. They are unlikely to be looking for a place to meet and eat biscuits. You never know though... there are those nice cupcake shops ☺

A mechanic isn't a car technician, an accountant isn't a financial expert and an airport isn't a gateway to the world when it comes to Internet searches.

You have to focus on using common language keywords if you want to attract the most visitors to your website.

Be specific. Use the words your customers use.

People just tend to use common language and terms for businesses when searching.

An accountant might give financial and business advice but they are more likely to get targeted clients by using keywords such as accountant, accountants, tax accountant and business accountant.

If they want to promote themselves as a financial advisor, my advice would be to set up a second topic-focused website to promote for that keyword and integrate related phrases like financial consultant and financial planner into the SEO.

Tip: You don't have to own only one website. It is extremely cost effective to own multiple websites that can be optimised for one major keyword to get better rankings.

If you try to use one website to be everything to everybody, you will probably fail to rank for any of your keywords. This is often the reason that businesses fail online. The just spread their content keyword focus too thin to have any effect on the search engine rankings.

You have to focus your onsite SEO into one major area. That area is the words you hear people use to describe what you do or sell when they're talking to you.

Look at the examples below:

Your Term	Online Search
Horticultural engineers	Gardener, landscaper
Most popular eatery	Restaurant, café
Property consultant	Real estate agent
Mortgage advisor	Mortgage broker, home loans
Marketing expert	Small business marketing, green marketing

The list above is just a series of examples. Before you chose the keywords for your business, you should do much more research. They do, however, show you how vastly different a customers language may be to your industry jargon.

Tracking your Rankings

Once you have edited your SEO, the next step is to wait until the search engines re-index your pages. But how will you know if your work is having an effect? You could sit there and type in a range of keywords to see where you rank but the results are affected by whether you're logged in to Google, where you are located, what device you're using and many other factors.

If you want true results, try using ranking software. There's a plethora of programs that can help you to track your ranking results. I personally prefer WebCEO. It's free for a single user.

Link: *http://ranking.mrwebmarketing.com*

One of the key features of this software is that you can load a large list of keyword phrases in, then set your country and a host of other settings like mobile ranking results. Once you press Start, you just sit back and it will go and interrogate the search engines, come back with your ranking positions and produce a simple to read report.

One of best functions is that the results are stored and over time you can graph the ups and downs to see how your work has affected the results. That data can then be compared with your traffic results.

When adding keywords to track, I also like to include local place keywords like SEO training Brisbane, SEO training Gold Coast, SEO training Melbourne so that I can see how a site might be ranking within those cities or suburbs. A business that services a group of suburbs might add all of them into the software to check their positions e.g. mechanic Ashmore, mechanic Parramatta, mechanic Wynnum.

If you are serious about getting better rankings, get serious about tracking them.

What is SEO success?

Traffic is the true indication of success with SEO. Having top rankings but no traffic indicates that you're optimised for the wrong keywords or your business may be too niche for the mass market.

That said, some people want to rank for specific keywords and as long as they own those #1 spots, they're happy. You might be targeting a highly specific search term which only brings 10 people a month, but each sale might be worth $1Million.

Traffic is great but.... Conversion is where the money is.

If you receive one visitor a day and convert that visitor, then you have obtained a 100% conversion ratio. If you receive a hundred visitors a day and you convert three you have obtained a 3% conversion ratio. This is where tracking becomes vitally important, more so than the actual ranking results.

If you don't track what happens as a result of changes you make, you won't know whether it worked or whether it had no effect. Without tracking, you won't even know if you're still sitting in the same spot.

Real marketers know every number: rankings, traffic, conversions, page visitors, most popular download, etc.

Measuring Your Successes With Analytics

There is no point in having a website if you don't track your metrics. Learn what traffic you're getting, where it's coming from, what words they're using to find you and what pages each visitor is looking at.

Good analytics allow you to make decisions about changes to your site - what you should improve and what you should remove.

Missing Key Information

If you do not have Google Analytics on your site then you're missing out on a great opportunity. It's completely free. It will integrate with your Google Adwords, with your Google Webmaster Tools and with your Google Places accounts. It will aggregate all the data together and... it costs nothing.

Analytics are the business metrics for your website. This information is extremely powerful. Why? Because it can show you where to spend your advertising budget. It can show you where new markets are emerging. It can show you which new pages to create to target the searches you are getting.

For example, you might have a page where you just mention that you supply Chocolate Frogs. Then you find out there are hundreds of people coming to your site who are looking to buy Chocolate Frogs even though they are only a small part of the confectionary range you carry.

With this information, you could go to your Chocolate Frogs page and rewrite it to say a lot more e.g. "We sell Chocolate Frogs and have a huge range of them. We have jelly filled centers, red ones, blue ones and pink ones". You could finish the page off by adding some clear images, including a video of someone eating a Chocolate Frog and placing links to your shopping cart so people can buy.

By doing these things, you can improve the information on that page and possibly increase your share of the online chocolate frog market.

Analytics gives you the information to make these decisions. You should always watch your stats otherwise, how are you going to know if your SEO is working if you don't know how many people are coming? There is no way to tell otherwise.

Sitemaps Help Google Rank You

Google has now taken to liking XML Sitemaps. A sitemap is a file that lists all the pages on your website and their addresses - their names and where they are located. It's done in a format called XML.

There's a range of tools available online if you just do a search for an XML site map creator it will create one for you that you can then upload to your site. Most content management systems have this built in. You can generally locate your sitemap if you type www.yourdomain.com.au/sitemap.xml.

Google has developed a free service it calls Google Webmaster Tools. You can submit your sitemap to it which will encourage Google to come and index your pages. This indexing will bring back all sorts of extra information and data which is different again to what you get from Google Analytics.

Your Gmail account is used as your login for Google Webmaster Tools and Google Analytics and Google Places. Everything Google is tied to that one address.

Bing also has Webmaster Tools that you should install on your website. You may find that Bing traffic may be better for your business. Their users may be a better fit for your products so if you can get better information and improve your rankings, you should take advantage of their gift.

Another Great Feature of Webmaster Tools

If you get malware, which is when you get viruses on your website, Google will shut down your site in their index. When you do a search, your listing will come up with a message underneath that says *malware found* and when someone clicks on it, they'll come to a page that says "WARNING: This site may harm your computer."

If you go to Google Webmaster Tools, it'll tell you which pages are infected. You can then go and clean those pages and kill the piece of code. Then through Webmaster Tools you can tell Google that you have fixed the problem and they will check and hopefully clear your site so you can get traffic again.

This feature alone is worth your time to install it. It has allowed me to get multiple sites back up and running quickly after they've been attacked. Previously, you had to wait till Google came back to your site weeks later.

Review

Most businesses will never fix their onsite SEO. They just don't get it finished because they run out of time or fail to understand how vitally important it is to their success. Just by following the tips in this chapter, you will put yourself ahead of 80-90% of other businesses.

Do your keyword research, fix your titles and meta tags, keyword match your content and track your results. Then repeat!

Key Points to Action:

- Conduct extensive keyword research.
- Fix your page titles and meta tags.
- Review and keyword match your content.
- Install Google Analytics and Webmaster Tools.
- Track your rankings with WebCEO.
- Repeat until you're at the top.

Steps To Take Today:

- Make a list of keywords people might use to find you or your products.

Steps To Take this Month:

- List all your pages in Google by searching for *site:www.yourwebsiteURL.com*
- Focus your thinking on your most profitable markets.
- Use Google Trends to do keyword research into these markets.
- Get a baseline ranking report using software – http://ranking.mrwebmarketing.com
- Optimise your website.
- Install your tracking code.
- Review rankings 2 weeks after optimization.

Case Study 1

Implementing SEO

Chiquel

At one time or another, every successful business started out as a simple idea in someone's mind. Creating a business is a magical process that's fueled with drive, determination and a need for bringing that idea into the real world.

As we all know however, not every business idea ends up turning into a profitable adventure. Have you ever questioned why some online businesses see massive success, while others go under before anyone even knows they exist?

In this case study, you'll see how one individual took an idea and turned it into a profitable online business in a very short period of time. This story is truly inspiring, as the business owner in this case didn't have any previous experience with running a successful online business.

The business owner also realised what type of business she should run due to her own personal battle with a health problem.

Read on and see how taking the proper steps in the beginning can help you achieve the level of online success that you desire. If this feel good story doesn't get you motivated to take charge of your website's search engine optimisation, then I don't know what will!

Introducing Chiquel

Just outside of Melbourne, Australia is Moonee Ponds. In Moonee Ponds, you can find Chiquel Salon and Fine Wigs. Owner Natalie, who was 21 years old at the time, realised that Australians didn't have a lot to choose from when it came to finding well-made wigs and hairpieces.

Natalie battles with alopecia; a disease that causes unexplained hair loss and she knew that there were others out there who'd appreciate being able to easily find and buy wigs online.

While one of Natalie's main goals was to help others like her who suffer from hair loss, she wanted to kick it up a notch. She also knew that there were people out there who were interested in buying wigs and hairpieces to simply change their look whenever they wanted to.

At the time, people were limited to mostly costume wigs that were of poor quality and didn't look natural when worn.

But how was this young and aspiring business owner going to find success selling online? When you have a physical store location, people can drive or walk by it and see the signs out front. When you're trying to take your business online, your store front is your website listing in the search engines.

The problem is that there are thousands or even millions of other stores in the search engines that want to share the same storefront space. In order to get noticed in the search engines, your store needs to be at the top of the first page of the results.

The Plan

Natalie turned towards traditional marketing tactics in regards to her salon and wig shop, such as taking out newspaper ads but she knew that she needed to do more when it came to her online store.

Newspaper ads and print advertisements weren't going to drive traffic to her website and she knew that. She also knew that if she wanted to make the most of her business, she needed to have a solid presence online.

Natalie realised that if she wanted her online business to be a success, then she needed to implement search engine optimisation (SEO). She realised this from very early on, but saw the need for it even more once her website was near completion and website traffic was essentially at a standstill.

As a business owner who was busy running a physical location, she knew that she needed help to complete her optimisation goals. Not only did she need help, but also she didn't want to wait years to start seeing orders come in from her online store.

Natalie enlisted experts for her search engine optimisation plan. The results? Putting it lightly, the results have been over the top and astounding.

The Results

Prior to SEO kicking in, the phone and email fronts were very quiet for online orders. Online business was not only non-existent, but also Natalie's website wasn't found anywhere near the top of the search engine results.

The situation isn't surprising at all. Remember, the 1st website result in Google gets roughly 56 clicks out of every 100 views. If your website isn't on the first page, silence can be expected. The majority of the business is going to the first three websites that show up in the search engines.

Fast forward to 3 months after Natalie's SEO campaign was in full swing and you could easily see what a difference optimisation made! In the short time period of 3 months, Chiquel.com.au made it to Google's 1st page of results for the highly competitive keywords of "wigs" and "wig". Those aren't long-tail key phrases, those are one word keywords!

Getting to page 1 in Google for very competitive keywords is great, but what did that mean for Natalie's business? It meant that the phones were ringing non-stop and orders were coming in left and right!

Chiquel went from having literally no visitors and no orders to a booming business, simply based on where the website was being found in the search engines.

Here are some more fantastic results that Natalie saw for her online wig store after SEO was implemented:

- Not only did SEO increase local online sales but it also increased worldwide sales.

- Customers are actually flying from locations around the world to visit Natalie's physical store location!

- After 6 months, Natalie saw her website traffic increase to around 2,000 visitors per month (from 0!)

- Being on the first page in Google also helped with referrals and word of mouth recommendations.

Considerations

Do you need to be a seasoned business owner or know everything about doing business online in order to be successful? Absolutely not! The success of Chiquel that's outlined above perfectly proves that if you know what you want to achieve, then anything is possible.

You don't need to have an education in business to start up a successful company; all you need is a good plan and the right people to stand behind you.

Imagine waking up one morning to see your website listed on the first page of Google's results for your preferred keywords. Then imagine logging on to your computer and seeing order after order pouring in or the phone ringing non-stop.

It'd feel pretty good wouldn't it? Of course it would! The best part is that search engine optimisation can easily make this scenario a reality.

Do you need to have an online store in order to benefit from SEO? Absolutely not! Every single type of website or online business can benefit from SEO. It doesn't matter if you're selling products and services or if you just want to drive more readers to your blog.

In order to get a higher amount of website traffic, you need more exposure and one of the best ways to achieve more online exposure is through SEO!

Conclusion

The difference between those who succeed and don't succeed when it comes to online businesses is that those who end up successful know how important exposure in the search engines is. Not only do they know how important it is, but also they make it one of their top priorities.

After realising the success that Chiquel has had due to utilising SEO, ask yourself: Do I want to see that kind of success for my online business or am I okay with where my business is at now?

If you're looking to take your website to the next level and stop letting it sit there doing nothing all day long, it's time to introduce your website to its new friend- SEO.

Success doesn't just happen all by itself- it happens when action is taken.

Whether you already have a website that's been underperforming or you're just starting to think up your next big online business idea, including a professional SEO expert as part of your plan is one of the best decisions that you and your business will ever make.

Link: *http://bit.ly/WemRHA*

Step 2

Build A Massive Link System To Your Site

Step 2: Build a Massive Link System To Your Site.

This is the point where 95% of businesses stop their SEO and consequently fail to get the best rankings in the search results.

It's common knowledge that it's good to have other websites linked to you. Google sees these as "votes of confidence" in the quality of your information, products or services.

What isn't common knowledge is that a large part of Google's search ranking formula seems to be focused on this. That makes this part of the SEO process EXTREMELY important.

If you decide to start an ongoing program of link building back to your site, you will be in the top 5% of people trying to sell online. If you continue for over 12 months, I venture to suggest you would be in the top 2%.

Almost no one takes this extra step and that's why SEO companies consistently get better ranking results for people than most businesses do on their own. They employ a regimented system of ongoing link building as well as a range of other techniques.

Why link?

It's like a vote of confidence.

Just say we're in a networking meeting and you knew me and that I was an online marketing specialist. Someone walks in and says to you, "I need some help with my website, I can't get it to rank" Like any helpful business owner, you say, "You need to talk to Brad Hauck." Then later on that they're talking to someone else and say, "Oh, I'm having trouble with my website." And they get the response, "You need to talk to Brad." Chances are that they will think, "I probably should have a chat to Brad. There's no cost to me but at least I might get an answer or help."

Google thinks the same way. Every one of the sites linking to you is seen as a vote of confidence that you're the expert in your area.

You need to keep building links. Link building is an ongoing process. *This is not something you do once.*

Google sees things you do once as a glitch. Their robots think, "Oh, a glitch, ignore that. Keep watching them, let's see what they do over time."

If you want to be rewarded by search engines you've got to be consistent over time.

Types of links

Surprisingly, structurally there is a range of different styles of links that you can build. The best and most "powerful" are the 1 way links. Followed by 3 way links and reciprocal links.

So What's the Difference?

1 Way Links are links that link one way, to your website. You don't link to them in return. In my experience, this is the best sort of link as the search engines see it as an indicator of your expertise in an area. The more sites you have linking 1 way to you, the more you look like the site that everyone says is the best for your topic.

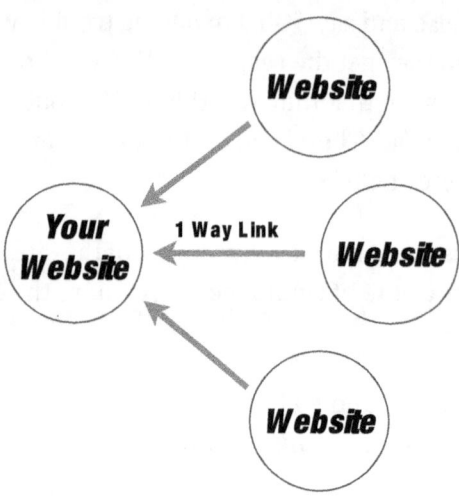

3 way links are similar to 1 way links except that they're normally constructed after negotiation with other site owners. You agree to link to Website 2 if they agree to link to Website 1 who agree in turn to link to your website.

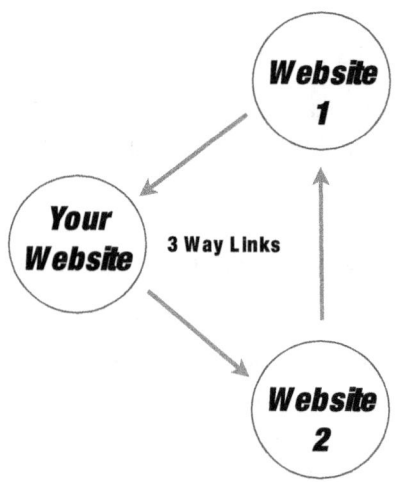

Most of the time, these links are more trouble than they're worth to do but if you have a group of local businesses who want to help each other, you can use this method so that you get better themed links.

Reciprocal links are links you get when you agree with another site owner to link directly to each other. It's a straight swap. Most SEO specialists support that these cancel each other out as far as search engine recognition but they can be highly successful for getting direct traffic from other websites.

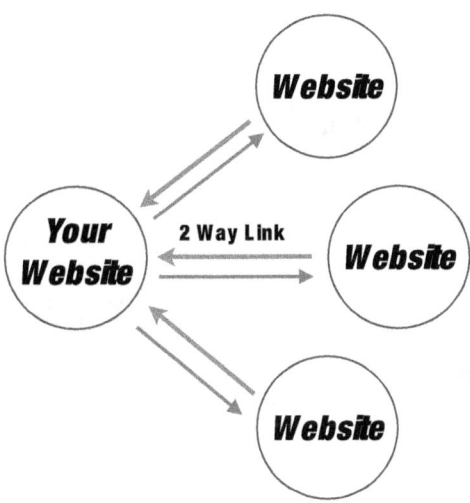

Linking Strategies

If you want the best results out of link building, you should plan out a basic link strategy. If you need quality 1 way links, you can also use mini websites that you own as part of your strategy. You can also build links to these sites to improve their importance. If you want to get even more into it, mini sites can have their own mini sites!

What ever you choose to do, draw out a basic plan and stick to it until you start to see results.

There are many sites that you can use for link building. Let's look at a few of the more effective types of links that you can build.

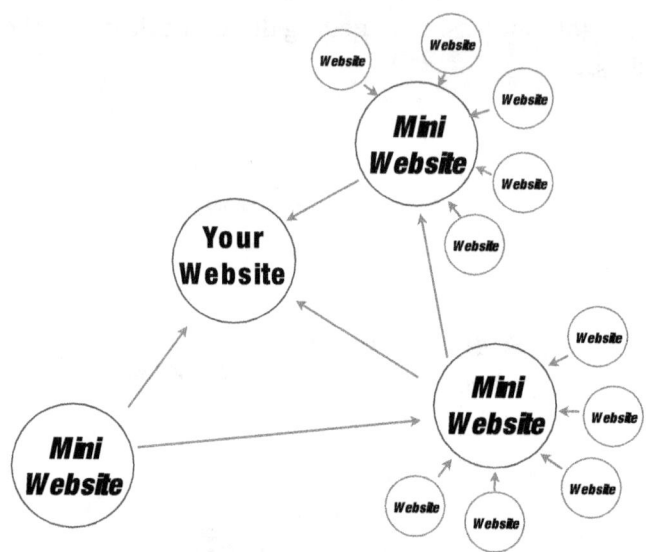

Local & International Directories

There are many local business directories that you can add your business to for free. Search for "business directory your-city" to find the ones closest to you. Once you have submitted your site to those, start searching for countrywide directories to submit to.

It's been my experience that there is only 1 directory that is really worth paying to be listed in. It costs $299 USD/year and it's Yahoo.

Most of the others are a waste of money. They get the traffic, they get your money and if you check your statistics, you'll find that you get almost no referrals from them. My experience is that they have a great sales pitch but that's about it.

If you do decide to try some of the paid directories, closely monitor your traffic, calls, sales, etc. and then make a decision at renewal time whether it's worth continuing. In most cases these sites will give you a free listing anyway. You can use a 1300 number to track your resulting calls. You can get a number that even records every call, number and time is you use my provider.

Link: *1300.mrwebmarketing.com*

Save your pennies...

Article Links

Writing a unique article of around 450 words and submitting it to article directories like ezinearticles.com is still one of the most effective ways to build links back to your website.

Your article should be written about the same topic as your main keywords. Personally I find it easier to write from a question so I often title my articles like this:

How does link building improve your search rankings?

Even after upheavals like the Google Panda update which affected article site's rankings, it is still well and truly worth your time.

There are literally thousands of article sites that you can submit to so you will never run out of places to build links. I suggest you start with the highest ranking ones (in Google), as they are the ones most likely to be indexed by the search engines first.

To get a link from your article back to your website, make sure you include one in your Bio when you submit. It's best to build the link into the text using your keywords.

If you're unsure how to insert a link, most article sites have short tutorials that explain it to you.

Social Bookmarks

Just like social networking sites, we also have social bookmarking sites and, for a while, they were thought of as the new search engines. How do they work? When you see a site you like, you bookmark it onto Digg or another social bookmarking site. The more people that bookmark it, the more votes the site gets and the higher it ranks in Digg's results. It's a bit like keeping your bookmarks or favourites online.

Google's +1 feature is its effort to incorporate some of the voting features of these sites into their search engine so don't forget to +1 your website and articles too. This tool will continue to grow in popularity especially if Google Plus, its new social network, takes off which it is now starting to do.

Social bookmarks get indexed quickly as the search engines are always looking for up to date content and people bookmarking interesting sites that they find as a shortcut to finding that content. There are loads of social bookmarking sites that you can bookmark your site on and each one counts as a link to you.

Press Releases

Online press releases can be a very powerful source of links. All you need to do is write a standard press release then submit it through the online press submission services. You can pay or play for free. Paid services tend to get better indexing and reach a wider, often more professional, range of syndication feeds including Google News and Associated Press.

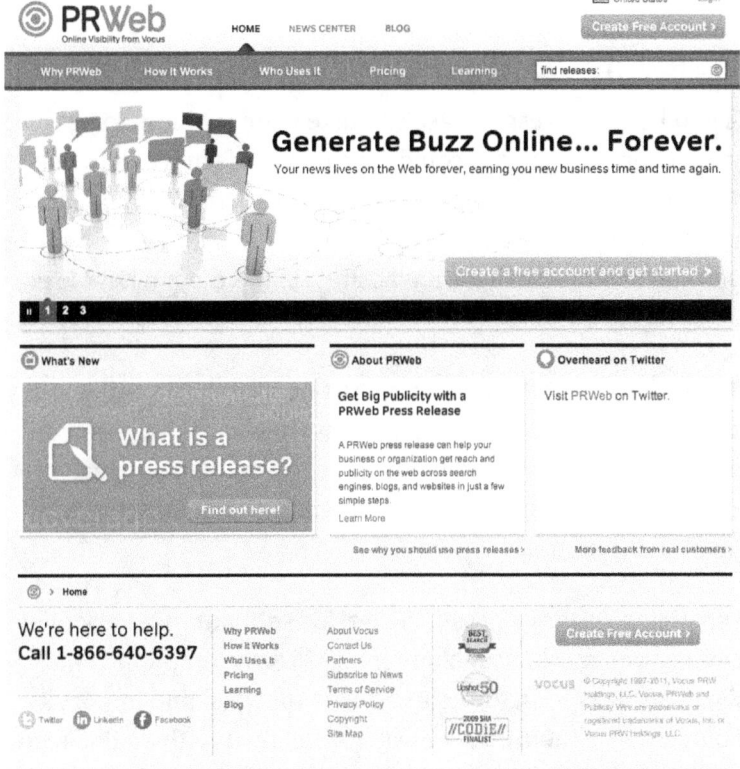

Unlike an offline press release, when you submit an online press release you are able to include links to your site, email addresses, videos, images and even social links to Facebook.

Every time your press release shows up on a feed or a news website, you get another link back to you. This can lead to tens of thousands of links in a very short time if you write something viral.

Most people think that leveraging the press is something that PR companies do, and that may be true offline but online anyone can submit a press release which can appear on thousands of websites. All of these websites will display your release and a link back to your business.

Welcome To The Power Of Syndication!

A good online press release can take your business to people you never thought you could reach. There is more than one story of releases being picked up by the mainstream media and being flashed to the whole world. How many stories have you seen about small local websites on the 6 pm news? I see at least one a week.

These days, a lot of people read the news online so all it takes is one journalist who's having a slow day to see your release and suddenly you'll find yourself being on the front page of News.com.au or another newspaper site, hopefully for positive reasons.

When you submit a press release, it's sent out by a variety of syndication methods including RSS (Really Simple Syndication) feeds. Anyone can take this feed and import its contents into their own website or follow it with an RSS feed reader.

RSS Feeds from your Website

Many sites such as blogs and CMS's have a built in RSS feed

that syndicates the posts and pages you add to your website. What does that mean for you? You can submit that feed URL to a whole slew of RSS search engines including Google to get them to list your content more quickly.

These sites are also places that people go to look for feeds to use on their own websites. If you include links in your content you can spread your message and a link back to you all over the world in minutes.

Get Read and Go Viral

Writing a good press release isn't about hyping your news up. If anything, you play it down and stick to the facts. You need to learn to write within a limited number of words. The most important part of this is the headline.

If your headline is no good, people wont read on and neither will an editor or journalist. Imagine how good your *BS detector* would be if you were reading hundreds of press release feeds a week.

Be precise and target your headline to your market. Instead of long winded statements like:

"Mrwebmarketing Releases Results Of 6 Month Survey That Shows 1 Million People Buy Products From Ads In Email Each Month in Australia"

Try something more precise:

"Survey Shows 1 Million People Buy From Emails Every Month"

Your headline must quickly convey the kind of information needed to capture the reader's attention.

If you haven't used press releases before, I suggest you search online for a company like PR Web to do your first one for you or hire a local specialist and submit via PR Web.

Profiling Yourself on Social Media

Today, with all the social media action, you obviously can't ignore setting up a profile for you and your business on each of the main social networking sites. Profiles from YouTube, LinkedIn, Facebook, Twitter and Google+ all get ranked on the search engines.

These are often personal profiles so you will need to include links to your business website if you want to get the most effect from them.

The quickest way to see what sites are ranking for you is to do a search for your name e.g. "Brad Hauck" and see what is showing up. If you don't see your listings for the sites mentioned above, go back and finish your profile and fan pages.

We'll look at social media in more depth later in the 7 steps.

How many links should you be doing a month?

I'd suggest upwards of 300 depending on the quality of the links. On the other side though, don't go out and start doing 1 million links a month. This shows up as an anomaly to the search engines and you will probably get penalised for it. Start at 300 and grow, if you wish to, over 6 months.

BTW the best sort of link is one from a site in the same industry as yours e.g. a construction company might have a link from a plumber's website.

You Can't Do It On Your Own.

Time is the biggest killer of good intentions. Most business people I know would love to do all of their marketing in-house but can't afford it. Let's take link building for example. It takes about 2-10 minutes to submit a new link depending on how practised you are. If you want to build 400 new links a month, that works out like this:

400 x 5 minutes = 2000 minutes (33 hrs. approx.)

33 hrs. X $25/hr. = $825

To be realistic, it will probably take most people 10 minutes to build a link which doubles the overall cost plus you need to find someone who will sit there and do that task all day every day. That's why most businesses don't do it.

How do you solve the problem?

Outsource the work or hire a company that can take care of that and all the other work for you.

Since 1996, I've only met a handful of companies that have successfully completed their SEO in-house. It's just not economical or cost effective!

I don't tell you this because I ran a company that did this sort of work, I tell you this because I know the truth. In the time it takes you to learn SEO and start building links, an SEO company will already have your rankings moving up.

If you do the onsite SEO yourself, hire someone to do the offsite link building. I recommend the team found at *links.mrwebmarketing.com* as I've worked with these guys for over 5 years and their work is effective and efficient. The same 400 links I discussed above would cost you less than $200.

What ever you decide to do in relation to link building, the most important thing to do is start and continues each month. Regular link building is rewarded handsomely.

Someone to Do It for You

If you're looking for a company to do all of your SEO, I currently recommend Promote SEO.

Link: *www.PromoteSEO.com.au*

Key Points to Action:

- Regular link building is ESSENTIAL for better rankings.

- Search engines like quality links to your site.

- Need to build a range of links.

- Put a plan in place to have links built.

- Build your social media profiles and link back to your website.

Steps to take today:

- Start building links from local business directories.

- Complete your SM profiles.

- Start your first article or hire someone through eElance.com.

Steps to take this month:

- Consider hiring a reliable link building team.

- Contact Promote SEO if you're time poor.

- Add link building into your monthly actionable tasks.

Case Study 2

Link Building

Stella Promotions & Owyak Bin Hire

I want you to think back to the time before the ability to market online became a reality. Before websites, blogs and social media were the big ways to market your products and services, you were left with traditional print marketing, television advertisements and word of mouth marketing. It's that last one, word of mouth marketing, that I want you to really think about for a moment.

With word of mouth marketing, people who liked your products or services would tell their friends, family and acquaintances about your business. A familiar person vouching for your business created an instant level of trust between the potential customer and your company.

The thought behind this process is that people generally believe that if one or more people trust and respect your business, then they'll feel more comfortable to trust your business as well. Word of mouth marketing is still relevant today.

Fast forward to the present day with a good majority of people turning to the Internet and the search engines to find the products and services that they're looking for. While Internet users can choose to speak to their friends and family to find a good company to do business with, simply searching online is quicker and more efficient.

But how do Internet users and the search engines know what websites to trust? If no verbal conversations are taking place, what online businesses can be trusted?

This is exactly where link building comes in and one of the many ways that it's beneficial! When a website links to your website, they're essentially vouching for you, your site and your business. It's saying "I trust this company enough to risk my reputation to link to them."

Consumers, Internet users and the search engines all value this sentiment. It's all about trust, and link building is one of the top ways that your website can earn trust across multiple boards.

Other benefits of link building include:

- Higher search engine placement
- More website traffic
- Higher conversion rates
- More exposure

Link building is part of search engine optimisation and it's one of the most important parts of the process. To back up this statement, the following two case studies will present you with evidence of what link building can achieve.

Introducing Stella Promotions

Stella Promotions sells promotional products to businesses in Australia. What makes this case so unique is that the company sells their products to other businesses in Australia. They're not a large worldwide company and they only sell to a small specific niche customer. Due to this, their search engine optimisation and link building needed to be kept on a local and national level.

The Plan

Partake in off-site optimisation strategies that focused on a few narrow key phrases, combined with local and national link building. Stella Promotions didn't have the option of using worldwide web directories for their link building strategy since it may not have helped their online campaign.

The Results

Stella Promotions is the perfect example of how a little link building can go a long way! After link building was completed, the website benefited from improved rankings in the search engines, an increase in website visitors and an increase in revenue.

All of this was possible because, through link building, Stella Promotions was able to connect with their niche audience. With other quality and relevant websites linking to them, they were also able to achieve higher search engine placement.

Considerations

What's very exciting about Stella Promotions and their success is that in their line of business, it's impossible to market to everyone simply because there are only select people and businesses that have a need for their products.

Traditional offline and online marketing techniques wouldn't have proven successful and would've been a waste of time. In some cases, all it takes is a little bit of link building to get the job done and see more money flowing in!

Introducing Owyak Bin Hire

When you think about search engine optimisation, link building and online marketing, a rubbish and recycling bin company in Wellington, New Zealand isn't likely to be the first thing that comes to mind! Even so, Owyak Bin Hire is the perfect example to show that even the most unlikely of characters can still greatly benefit from link building!

The Plan

Owyak Bin Hire wanted their website to be listed on the first page of Google's results for several key phrases that are relevant to their company and the services that they provide. After realising the proper key phrases that they should focus on, link building was started, mostly focusing on directory submissions. Remember, link building can greatly boost the chances of a website being listed on page 1 of the results in the search engines. Was this the case for Owyak Bin Hire?

The Results

It certainly was! Owyak Bin Hire saw excellent results through link building efforts! The following key phrases made it to page 1 of the search results in Google:

- Bin hire rates
- Rubbish skips for hire
- Front loading bins for hire
- Bin Hire Wellington
- Book a bin Wellington

That's just the short list of the key phrases that Owyak Bin Hire was able to achieve page 1 results for in Google through the act of link building! On top of the page 1 search rankings, the company also saw a 30% increase in website visitors in the month following link building efforts. Imagine your website's traffic increasing by 30% in one month!

Considerations

Is every person in need of booking a rubbish or recycling bin? Of course not! But this is exactly why it was very important for Owyak Bin Hire to place on the first page of the search results. Rubbish removal and recycling is a very small niche market that only a select number of people are looking for.

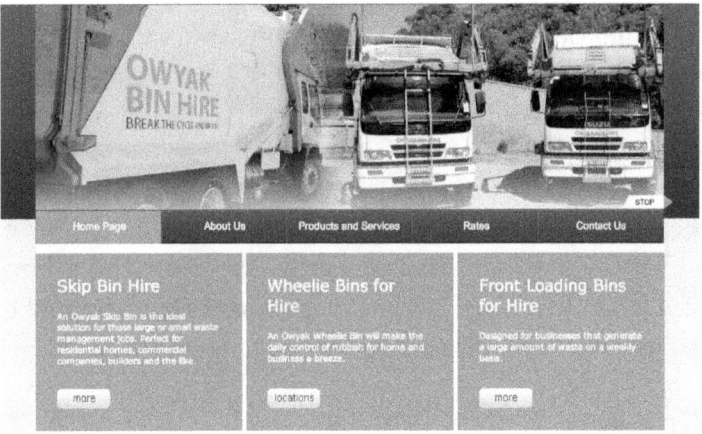

If a website is buried at the bottom of the search engine results in a very small niche market, the chances of seeing an increase in website visitors or an increase in business is pretty much zero.

Summary

While link building is exceptionally beneficial no matter what kind of business you have, the benefits for small businesses can easily be seen in the two case studies above. Large corporations that are known on a worldwide level, often receive direct Internet traffic because a lot of people are aware of their brand and they're also searched for by name in the search engines.

When you own or operate a small business, Internet users are most often going to find you by searching for specific words or phrases that are relevant to what they need or want. If proper optimisation and link building is done and your website shows up on the first page in the search engine results, your business is going to be raking in the benefits.

On the flip side of the coin, if these steps aren't taken, then when users search for keywords or phrases, they're going to end up seeing another businesses website at the top instead of yours.

As an added bonus, efforts from link building are often seen in a very short period of time. A good example of this is how Owyak Bin Hire saw a 30% increase in website traffic in the first month after link building was completed!

Who wouldn't love that type of increase?

Link: *http://bit.ly/128jepS*

Step 3

Create A Social Media Explosion

Step 3: Create a Social Media Explosion

Creating a social media explosion isn't just about exploding onto hundreds of social media sites. It's about ensuring that you engage with people.

Social media is the new black and everyone's talking about it.

You'll read every day about how you can use it in your business yet most business owners see no $$$ at all from it when you talk to them about it. Often, their constant self promotion and selling quickly kills off any following they have built and any further interest in what they might know that could be helpful.

A common myth about social networking is, "if you build it, they will come", which is a load of garbage. It would be more truthful to say, "If you get to know me, engage in meaningful conversation, interact with me and show me you care, I might trust and follow you."

Don't be fooled, there is a pile of hype surrounding social media so high you might never get through it to the truth. Which, BTW, is that there is no #1 social media site to use and there is no right way to succeed using it. It all depends on your business and what angle you take to reach your audience. There's no "silver bullets" to success with social media.

The most successful social media campaigns have targeted a specific niche of the market and tried to engage with it through humour, education, free giveaways, competitions, etc. By aiming at a small group of people, they are able to get their message passed on to other friends who share similar interests or are raving fans.

What Does This Mean for Your Business?

We all know social media is absolutely essential today.

Why? From a search engine point of view, Google's looking for a social media footprint. They're looking to see that you've got a profile on the main social media sites. They're counting that towards your rankings.

On the other side, you want to be in social media because that's where the people are. It's where you can get recommended and that brings people who are hot leads rather than just cold leads to your business.

Think about who your target clients are. What do they share in common? Is it a love of cars? They don't like to pay full price? They've all been 'stung' by an unscrupulous local company? What? Once you know what that thing is, you have a place to start planning your social strategy... and it's an ongoing campaign NOT a once-only activity.

Once you know who and how you're going to target with your campaign, you can plan your processes and set targets to achieve. There is no point in using social media unless you set goals. Don't use it just because everyone else is.

Why? Because you can bet they probably have no idea what they're doing or why they're doing it except to say that they started because everyone else was doing it. You need to, at the very least, try social media.

That's not exactly a great reason to start a new marketing effort.

Choosing the Right Social Media Site

In the social media world, there are the big three: Facebook, LinkedIn and Twitter. But in the background, quickly growing is Google Plus. The fact of the matter is that most people can't do all of them at once.

I recommend that you try them all and choose the one that you like to use. Myself, it's currently Facebook but I'm also active in working on LinkedIn. I like the way it works. For other friends, it's Twitter whereas business friends often prefer LinkedIn. You'll find me at:

- facebook.com/mrwebmarketing
- twitter.com/mrwebmarketing
- au.linkedin.com/in/mrwebmarketing
- Google+ - http://bit.ly/Y4PL9v

Or just search for me by name ☺

Another site you may not know of is Ning. Ning is a place where people can set up their own social media network. You can start your own social media site so *yourname.ning.com* or you can pay and have your own domain added.

What you'll find at Ning is what I call, "centric social media sites". These are networks like mummy-centric sites built for mums to interact. If you're looking for a specific market like mums then you might find there's actually a separate social media site setup specifically for that group of people.

Rather than wasting your time on Facebook where your market might be all over the place, you can go in and visit one social network and save yourself a lot of time.

Making Your Favourite Site Work For You

Every site has its own individual functions so get to know them.

If you want to use Twitter, get to know how to use DM, # and RT plus the other shortcuts that allow you to keep involved in a conversation, share things you like and comment to other people directly. If you want to learn more about Twitter, my 21 Days to Twitter book and blueprint will help.

Link: *twitter.mrwebmarketing.com*

If you're going to build traffic, you have to be involved. Research shows that tweeting 22 times a day is the optimum number of tweets. Personally, I can't keep that up. I just can't do 22. I think that is kind of in the fanatical range ☺

If you like Facebook, learn to use the Like, Share, Comment links to express your thoughts and opinions. If you're in a hurry, a Like is quicker than a comment but lets people know you agree with them.

With Facebook, if you're running a Page, try to put new information, links or images at least once a day and if people comment, comment on their comment because that then brings them back.

Why? Because Facebook alerts people that you have commented on their remarks which draws them back into the conversation. These alerts go directly to their smartphone, email and desktop depending on how they have things set up.

If you want to learn more about Twitter, my 21 Days to

Facebook book and blueprint will help.

Link: *fb.mrwebmarketing.com*

LinkedIn users can also take advantage of the Like feature, commenting, answers and company pages. But, if you're going to use LinkedIn, the real power is in the groups. This is where all the action is. Find a topic you love, get involved and follow up others' comments on your input.

Creating A Social Explosion

The quickest way to explode your social media reach is to get involved in conversations and groups in a positive, helpful way. If your input is useful and helps solve other people's problems, you quickly appear as the expert.

As the expert, people will turn to you when they need help offline because they will remember you. Think of it as putting money in the bank for a rainy day. Build your intellectual bank so that when someone needs your skills or services, they will come back to you directly to get your help.

It's a well known fact that if you've got a LinkedIn group or a Facebook fan page and it's not active, that you should:

- go and find everyone's questions
- write an answer to each question
- then ask the person a question back.

I've seen many people reactivate pages and groups just by doing that. That's all they do... sit there, answer what they thought and then ask the other person a question back and that brings the people back. It's a very easy technique.

In simple steps:

- Sign up to the site.
- Fill out a complete profile including photo and links to your website. Make it interesting.
- Find your friends first and join them.
- Upload your contact list from your email program.
- Find groups or fan pages around topics you love.
- Read through and get a feel for the attitude/style of the members.
- Start to make comments on other's questions and comments. Keep them light and friendly.
- Start to ask questions from the group. Respond to those people who answer.
- Friend those who you build a relationship with.
- Maybe start your own group, topic or fan page.
- Invite your friends or followers to join you.

Automating Your Status Updates

When you decide which one your favourite is, you can use software like dlvr.it to take a feed from the social site you like and share it with the other sites automatically. Yes, you read correctly. You can take your work from one site and feed others instantly without ever having to go to them.

All you need to do is set up an account on each, add those details to your dlvr.it account and "hey presto" all your status updates are done when you post to your one favourite social site.

To make this work even more efficiently, you can take an

Really Simple Syndication (RSS) feed from your blog or website so that every time you write a new page or post, dlvr.it sends that out for you. If you do this, all you need to do is concentrate on adding new content to your site.

Using tools like blogs, dlvr.it and Hootsuite, you can automate a lot of your posting up front.

If you're using automatic posting, I think you need to see it as a footprint or link building exercise. It works best if done so that it pulls people back to your blog.

If you can't do it all the time, use a social media manager to manage and interact on your behalf.

These people specialise in social media campaigns for businesses and putting your plan into place so you get great results.

Many Profiles

Make sure you complete personal & business profiles on all of the social media sites.

Why? Because when you create a profile, you create a link back to your website and the social media sites rank highly. If you type your name in, you'll probably find that your website comes up first, followed by LinkedIn, followed by Facebook, followed by twitter. They're the highest ranking sites.

It's reputation management. If you can hold the highest ranking sites and having a profile that shows on page 1 of the search engine results then you can save yourself a lot of time in reputation management.

I do a lot of work in this area protecting and building against damage. This is one way to start the process by creating profiles. By the way, there's hundreds of social media sites not just 3 or 4 so don't just limit your profiling to a few. Go to town on this!

Key Points to Action:

- Sign up to all the major social media sites.
- Create a profile and company page on each.
- Start posting daily.
- Connect with your contacts
- Choose the site that works best for your business and "work it".

Steps to take today:

- Fill out your complete profiles on Facebook & LinkedIn.
- Upload your email database to LinkedIn.

Steps to take this month:

- Try Ning.
- Join 10 groups on LinkedIn.
- Like 10 Facebook pages from local businesses.

Case Study 2

Social Media

Aquabumps and Teusner Wine

While social media platforms may grow and change, the social media explosion is here to stay. You've heard that social media is a large part of being successful online, but the proof is always in the pudding. Why invest time into something when you're not absolutely certain that it'll work?

Not only does social media work for businesses, but also these two case studies go to show how you can use social media to start a business even when starting a business was never your intention.

Introducing Aquabumps.com

Aquabumps.com wasn't started to make money online- but somehow, one surfer found himself running a legitimate and successful online business due to a few pictures that he took of Bondi Beach.

Every morning, the owner of Aquabumps.com would go out to Bondi Beach and take a picture. While the images taken are striking, the owner wasn't taking them with the intent to sell them. Actually, the only thing that he did with the photographs at first was email them to a few of his friends when he felt that his friends might need a little pick me up.

Then, all of the sudden, he ended up with a massive email following. I am not speaking of a few hundred email sign ups from people wanting to see the pictures, I'm talking 40,000 people! Realising that blasting out 40,000 emails every day might not be time efficient, even if automated, the owner of Aquabumps.com opted to start posting the pictures on his Facebook page.

Much like the results he saw from emailing the pictures, his following on Facebook quickly jumped to over 20,000 people

7 Steps to Getting More Business Online in Less Time!

and continued to grow! This is an extremely high number of people, especially since there wasn't any active marketing going on to drive followers to his Facebook page.

The Plan

The most fascinating aspect of this case study was that this person didn't have some gigantic plan to make money online; it just happened to turn out that way!

But then something strange started to happen...

As the followers of the Facebook website grew, so did requests for prints of the photographs that the Australian surfer took. Nearly every time a new photograph was posted on Facebook, there was at least one person asking how much prints are or how they could buy a copy of the picture.

A blog, a website and a massive photography portfolio later, the owner of Aquabumps.com not only has himself a very lucrative business, he has also amassed a social media following that is helping to sustain his business.

The Results

As of today's date, Aquabump's Facebook following has increased to over 70,000 people! On top of the Facebook following, his blog is quite popular as well, often receiving numerous comments and interactions every time a post is made. So he has a popular Facebook page and blog, but how does that equal success?

Aquabump.com has used Facebook and his blog to interact

76

with people and keep their interest. As the interest has built up, so have the sales from his photographs. His beach photographs have actually become so popular that poor Bondi Beach isn't getting the attention that it used to! The photographer now travels the world photographing beaches for a living! Who wouldn't love to have that job? I know I would...

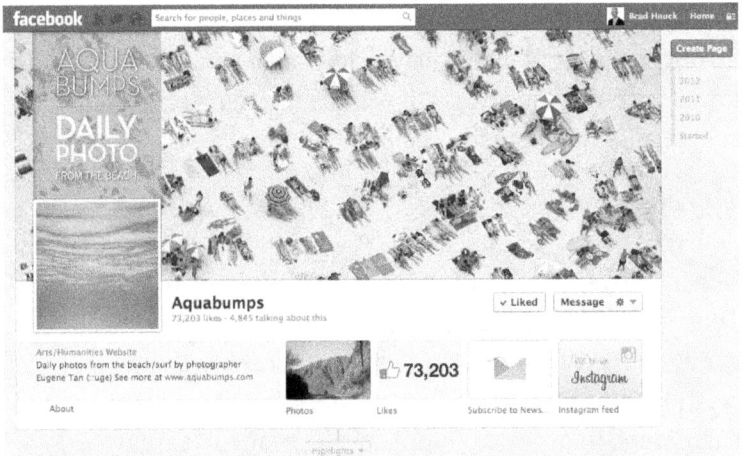

The beach photography business that a surfer ended up starting unknowingly is fetching thousands of dollars per print. The photographs also have their own gallery located in Bondi Beach which is appropriate of course, since that's where it all began. Due to social media, one surfer with a camera has found his niche and to think that most of it was basically accidental!

Considerations

If one surfer can see this much success from utilising social media to garner interest about his photographs, imagine the results that can be seen when social media is used intentionally! To see the effect when intent is present, let's take a quick look at another business, which also saw success from implementing social media.

Introducing Teusner Wine

Teusner Wine is located in Australia's Barossa Valley and they have three employees. One of those employees, who happens to work in the marketing department took notice that Lance Armstrong was using Twitter to spread his Live Strong message all over the world. Lance Armstrong gained a new Twitter follower that day, but something else spectacular happened as well.

The Plan

The employee saw a potential in Twitter for marketing Teusner Wine and the company came up with a goal to promote their business on Twitter in order to build relationships with current customers and also with potential customers. In order to complete this goal, the employee created a Twitter account for Teusner Wine and then he started searching for wine related terms on Twitter.

Through this process, they were able to find and connect with other people who were conversing about wine- those who already had an interest in wine related subject matters.

The Results

Teusner Wine now receives more wine tours than they were receiving pre-social media. Website traffic has also increased, plus:

- People from around the world are contacting them to see where they can purchase the wine

- Teusner has been able to build trust with their customers and potential customers by the way they engage with them on Twitter

- The company is receiving valuable feedback from customers and potential customers that has been helping them strengthen their business

Considerations

Teusner Wine was lucky enough to have an employee who works in their marketing department handle their social media campaign. While the company has seen very positive results from their social media efforts, not every business is going to have a person who can create and manage a successful social media campaign.

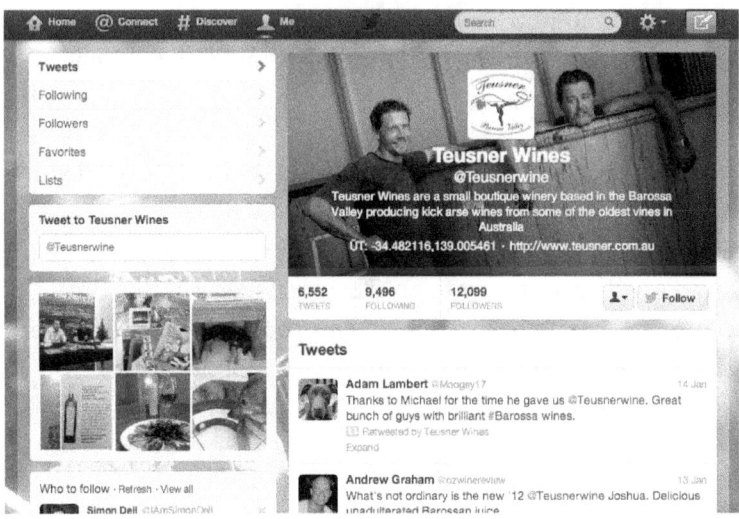

Don't fret however, as no matter what size or type of business you have, professional social media management is always an excellent option. It's also important to remember that social media marketing and traditional marketing are two very different sides of the profession and getting professional advice is always suggested.

Previous to watching a race on television, Teusner Wines had no intention of using social media to help boost their online and offline presence. As you can see however, a little bit of social media can go a very long way if used properly.

Summary

What you have above are two very different social media case studies. One person found himself in business online on accident by simply taking pictures of a beach and sharing them through email and Facebook with his peers.

Another business found social media via a sport that one of their employees was interested in. No matter how social media is found however, one thing can be said: Both businesses saw increased success by using social media for their business endeavors.

Where do you want your business to be in the future? If you want to see an increase in sales and build better relationships with customers and potential customers, then social media is one way to go! There's never a better time than right now to utilise the power of social media and take your business to the next level.

Links   *http://bit.ly/XQVr6O*

http://bit.ly/XIUX24

Step 4

Give Something Away To Build A List.

Step 4: Give Something Away to Build a List

Most businesses underestimate the power of a good list or database of people who might buy or have used their services in the past. Anyone who understands and applies this knowledge knows that there's millions of dollars in a list that is cultivated and worked regularly.

A list of names and contact details that just sits on your computer isn't worth the electronic ink it's written in.

Lists can take many forms: email, Facebook fans, twitter followers, direct mail, SMS and more. You don't have to use just one of them but working multiple lists can be demanding so I suggest you pick one or two that you like and work them hard. SMS is great for "in country" but Twitter might be better for worldwide.

In my opinion, the best list is the one that is easiest for people to subscribe to. For example, to join an email newsletter list, you have to type in your email address, submit and you're on the list.

But, statistics show that if you make people verify (double opt in) their email address by clicking on a link in an email, you achieve a higher level of readership and action from your readers.

On Facebook for excample, to become a fan, you just click the Like button. There's fewer steps, so less chances of someone deciding it's too hard to subscribe.

With that being said, you might find your market prefers or responds better to email. It's up to you to find that out.

Remember, success online is built around "test and improve". Test your different list types then make a decision.

How do You Build a List?

The first thing you need to clearly understand is that to build a list, you have to give something away. It might be a free product or service, a discount or a loss leader item. It often depends on what the lifetime value of a new client is to your business.

If you run a business where each new client is worth $500 a year to you, you can probably afford to give away a $100 saving on their first purchase or, if you were a mechanic for example, you might charge for parts only, labour free.

Mal Emery talks about the act of "giving away a part of a profit that you don't have to make a sale that you didn't have".

Let me explain that.

Most businesses won't give up a part of their profit from a sale to encourage people to buy from them. If they don't buy, you make NOTHING but if they do buy your offer, you still make a % of the profit.

If you sell a product for $400 and 25% is profit, you get $100 for each sale.

0 sales X $400 (25% profit) = $0

BUT

10 sales X ~~$400~~ $350 = $3500 which equals $500 profit.

That's $500 profit in your pocket compared to $0.

Work out what you are willing to give up to get a person to give you their details and their permission to contact them regularly. You had better make it a very juicy offer in these days of advertising inundation!

What Else Can You Give Away?

There are a range of gifts that you can give away. Here are just some that I have come up with quickly that you could email or snail mail to someone easily:

- Industry inside information

- Tips booklet

- Whitepapers

- 20 minute video

- 45 minute audio

- 1st chapter of your book

- Samples

- Coupon or discount card

- Worksheets or timesaving tools

- Free consultation voucher (phone or Skype)

- Invitation to a free webinar

The list is endless. You need to interview your market and find out from them what they would respond to best. Alternatively, try a few different offers and see which gets the most email sign ups. You can even split test it!

Working With Your List

You need to put a plan into place about how you're going to follow up your list regularly. Do you use a newsletter, social media updates, video updates, what?

As an example, Virgin Australia understands their audience. People like me, who join their Facebook fan page (a list in disguise), want cheap airfare offers from them... simple. So they keep those offers coming but they vary where they're for and what time they post so that you take the time to read them. They also mix up other news and tips with those updates.

If you have no plan for interacting with your list, there is **no point** in taking the time to build one. A list that isn't contacted for 6 months is dead list. You've lost their interest and focus. Which brings me to another point. A list has a life. It's generally only hot for a relatively short time because people's interests change quickly.

You need to get those people buying from you and continue to add new people or you will have to start from scratch again.

Layout a plan that instigates regular content being sent out. Make sure the content is compelling, educational or encourages thought.

Implement your plan following a schedule to ensure that you keep your list interested, involved and you in front of their eyes.

Make offers to the list at a rough ratio of 5:1 – 5 tips to 1 offer.

Helpful Software To Build Your List

There is a huge range of software now available to help you manage your list and to contact it. They start from your basic email program through to fully integrated email/SMS systems with social media plugins. I'd suggest that you start with something simple like an email list and use the free Mailchimp.com.

I've been using it for years and they allow you to send upwards of 2000 bulk emails to your list every month. If you need more, which most businesses won't, you can buy upgrades. You can upload your own list, set up an email newsletter template (or use one of theirs) and send at the click of a button. It's simple with a little practice.

One of the best features of modern email marketing systems is their integration with social media. Many companies write small plugins that add functionality to tools like MailChimp. If you're looking for additional services, you just get their tool and plug it in.

SMS is a great example of this. You can import all of your clients' details then either send them your newsletter or a short SMS all from the one website quickly and efficiently.

What to Send to Your List

Most people start by building an email list because they can collect addresses from business cards and website subscriptions. If you're in business, people will be interested in what you do and what specials you're running so keeping them up to date is essential for building your brand.

A "newsletter" is the easiest place to start because the layout gives you room to include all of the above. But you don't have to always use the standard layout. You can do online postcards, video newsletters and RSS newsletters that compile the latest 5 articles from your blog and send them out automatically for you.

Don't ever get stuck with a boring newsletter if you want to experiment. Remember, you can track open and click thru rates so you'll know if it works better for you or not.

Writing content that gets read

You can make a big difference to your read rates by following some simple principles when preparing to send a newsletter, special offer, tips or information to the people on your list.

It doesn't matter whether you're using an email list, Facebook fan page, twitter or blog, these will still apply. To get the best results, you need to study some basic copywriting skills.

5 Tips to Increase Read Rates

I learnt these when writing the AssociatePrograms.com newsletter with Allan Gardyne. Believe me, when you have a huge list you can easily see what your readers like and click on.

- Always use a headline as the title of your email or post.
- Never paste the first paragraph of your article into your newsletter then link to it. Write an original teaser paragraph to get their interest.
- Use a similar layout every time. People like familiarity.

- People love stories and case studies which illustrate your point.

- Never leave it till the last minute to write unless you write well under pressure. It brings out the worst writing in most people.

You Must Build a List

The value of a good list can't be underestimated.

Did you know that some marketers have email lists of well over 2 million people? That gives them a phenomenal reach when they send out their opinions, information and product offers! Imagine if you had 2 million people who were interested in what you do on your list.

How do you get a message out to people about a new product or service? Your list. How do you invite clients around for holiday drinks? Your list. What if you need some feedback on an idea? Ask your list.

Having 200 – 200,000 people on a list opens up so many possibilities and promotional opportunities. Just imagine if you had 10,000 local business owners on your list... even a 3% response to an offer would result in 300 sales! And, you could do that month after month!

Start today. Get all those business cards you've collected and add the name and email to your Mailchimp account and get a list going. Every time you go networking, add them to your list. Before long, you'll have quite the profit producer!

Key Points to Action:

- You must have a list.
- Divide your contacts up by how they like to be contacted.
- Send a regular newsletter style email.
- Check your list if it's older than 6 months.
- Don't waste all those contacts.

Steps to take today:

- Sign up to Mailchimp.com.
- Collect all the business cards you can find and add to Mailchimp.

Steps to take this month:

- Start your list.
- Prepare and send a newsletter.
- Track your responses.
- Clean your list of old emails / bounces.

Case Study 4

List Building

Black Ice Sunglasses

One thing that's essential to know about list building is that when you have a list, you have people who are already interested in your products or services. Think about it-people are very protective over their information these days.

If a person is willing to give you their email address and other details, then they're giving you those details because they want to hear from you! If you have a large list, then you have hundreds or even possibly thousands of people who are interested in what you're selling or providing.

If you decide to give something away for free, won't people just enter their details in order to receive the free product or service and then never buy anything from the company?

There's always going to be those who simply want something for nothing and that'll never change. Even so, it doesn't mean that you'll never make a sale off of your list building efforts if you opt to give something away to help you build your list-matter of fact, you'll more than likely see the opposite result.

When people want a free product or service and they enter their details, they do so in order to get something for free, but they wouldn't even want the free item if they didn't have an interest in the products or services that you offer.

For example, if you offer a free copy of a book that you wrote, people aren't going to enter their details to get a copy if they weren't interested in what the book was about. If consumers opted to get every free or discounted product out there, every person's home would be cluttered!

To reinforce this point, this next case study shows you how list building can be an awesome marketing tool and it may even give you an idea or two about what your company can possibly do to get your list building started. The best part?

Your website doesn't even have to be in tiptop shape to do what this company did or to see the results from it!

Introducing Black Ice Sunglasses

Black Ice Sunglasses (Black Ice Retail) is an online retail shop from New South Wales. On their website, they sell sunglasses, reading glasses, hats and watches. The company isn't some large retail chain, big box store or luxury retailer; they sell items in the 4 categories listed at reasonable prices. The audience that Black Ice markets to falls between the young teen to the young adult.

At the time in 2010, Black Ice didn't have a website that was worthy of building an email list from. Since first impressions are so important, the company needed to find a way to reach their target audience and build a list without having to rely on their website to help them out in the process.

The Plan

Black Ice wanted to start building a list so that they had a list of potential buyers to market to for when they had their summer sale. They decided that they wanted the demographic of their list to be females between the ages of 13 and 20.

Given their products and price point, narrowing down who they wanted to market to would help them be more successful with conversions. There's absolutely no sense in marketing to people who aren't going to have an interest in the products or services that your company is offering.

The list building plan for Black Ice was two-fold: The first step was finding a way to reach their specific demographic and to do so, they chose to place an ad in a magazine aimed towards the same demographic. The second they took was to target their demographic through Facebook advertising.

Along with these two steps, a separate landing page was also created so that it'd be more enticing than their website was. Remember, first impressions mean everything, even when marketing or list building online.

Back to giving away things for free, Black Ice actually offered those who signed up for their email list two things! The first thing was a chance to win a free pair of sunglasses and the second thing that subscribers received was a discount coupon that they could immediately use towards a purchase after signing up.

While they were giving something away for free, one pair of sunglasses isn't going to break the bank. The plan was to develop new customer relationships for future sales but due to the coupon code, it also encouraged immediate sales!

The Results

Through their list building efforts, Black Ice was able to start seeing almost immediate results. Prior to the Facebook campaign being launched, their list had already started to grow by leaps and bounds just from their magazine ad placement offering the chance to win a free pair of sunglasses and a discount coupon code!

Black Ice has seen a large volume of subscribers sign up to be on their list through these techniques. Their plan to build a list of people to market to for their summer sunglasses sale worked perfectly for that purpose and beyond.

Remember- once a person is on your list, they're on it unless they decide to opt out of it. Due to this, not only was Black Ice able to use the list for the summer promotion, but they were also able to use it for all future promotions and news that they wanted to tell people about.

Considerations

What's really neat is that this company didn't do a large give away of any sort. They kept what they were giving away to be manageable and reasonable; something that wouldn't dip far into their budget and risk their financial gains.

There's a myth that if you want to get a large number of subscribers to your list, then you need to do a massive give away but that's simply not true. Black Ice is a small company and giving away a pair of sunglasses for every person who signed up just wasn't a feasible option but they found a way to get subscribers without giving everything away.

The key to list building for any business is to reach those who are going to be the most likely to buy your products or services. Each type of business has a different type of demographic that they need to be marketing to.

If your business isn't aimed at the younger generation, then what Black Ice did to build their list might now have been as effective. It's all about finding out how you can connect with people and build your list from there.

The truth is that there are so many ways to build a list of email addresses for potential buyers! What's even better is that many of the options that you have for building up your email list are completely free. Due to the low cost of list building, it's perfect for small businesses and businesses that don't have a huge budget for advertising.

Summary

The benefits of list building are extreme. Yes, you get email addresses or contact details for people who have an interest in what you're selling, but you really get so much more! Take a look at some of the other benefits that your business can bring to life through list building:

Your list works for you 24/7! When you have a list and are able to email market from it, the emails you send obviously go to the people who signed up, but they also go beyond those people. With every email you send to your list, there's a chance that those who receive it will then forward it on to other people that they know!

Your website traffic can increase! If you're giving something away or holding a contest to build your list, that's going to generate interest from Internet users. A person who signs up may tell other people, which means that more people will be visiting your website. Website traffic will also increase when you send out emails to your list.

When done correctly, list building and email marketing can help create trust between potential customers and your company. It provides you with a platform to interact with customers on a more personal level.

When you list build and email market, you'll never have

another promotion go unnoticed! What good is a sale if no one knows about it?

The best part is that list building can work for any type of business. You don't need to sell products or services to benefit from list building; it's a good avenue to explore even if your only goal is to get more people visiting your blog or online magazine.

It's time to get going and let email start working for you and your business today! All you need is a creative idea to generate interest and then all you have to do is sit back and watch your list of potential customers grow.

Link: *http://bit.ly/UBwpes*

Step 5

Publish, Publish, Publish.

Step 5: Publish, Publish, Publish.

You can never have enough content on your website. 10 pages listed in the search engines is better than 1 because it increases your chances of being found. Think of it this way: you're more likely to catch more fish in a big net than you are using a single fishing rod.

More pages = more keyword combinations = get found for more searches = more leads

Once they have launched their website, most businesses fail to add new keyword focused, text content pages on a regular basis.

Note that I said keyword focused.

This is essential. Just adding random content is generally a waste of time.

In Step 1, you looked at the importance of SEO. SEO is an "all the time" skill not a one-time activity. Every time you write for the web, you need to have SEO and keywords in mind.

Never underestimate the power of publishing content to your website. Recently I bought a keyword focused domain Wordpressaholic.com.au, set up a simple site and started publishing unique articles 3-5 times a week on it. I did no link building other than to submit the site and it's RSS feeds to the search engines.

Within 1 month I was seeing 10-20 visitors a day and that grew to more than 50-100 a day within 3 months purely by adding new theme/keyword focused content. The site has hundreds of top 10 rankings worldwide including some quite competitive ones.

Styles of Publishing Online

There are multiple ways of publishing online:

- Web pages
- Videos
- Press releases
- Social networking
- Twitter
- Article submissions
- MP3 Podcasts
- Ebooks
- PDF files
- Word docs
- And more...

All of these types of publications get indexed in the search engines and you can search for them. Try searching for the following phrase on Google:

"business plan template filetype:doc"

Look at that... ready to edit business plan templates! You'd be amazed at what you can find using this sort of advanced search. You'd also be amazed at the amount of extra traffic it's possible to gain by adding files to your site in multiple formats especially if they're usable tools. Some Content Management Systems (CMS) can do this automatically.

Adding New Pages

You need to deliberately plan the addition of new pages to your website. Look at the pages you already have and think about whether they could be broken down into sub pages containing more specific information and photos about your products or services.

It's not uncommon to find a business website where they list all their services on one page. If you link off this list to a new page for each service, you not only create many new pages, you provide more detail that allows your visitor to make an informed buying choice.

Ensure that Your Content is Original.

Duplicating someone else's work is not only stealing, but you won't be rewarded by the search engines over the long term. They prefer unique work.

You won't be penalised for copying but you won't be rewarded either. You will be rewarded for original articles. Besides, do you want someone recognising that they have read this page somewhere else? How would that look for you? If you do want to use a good article written by someone else to illustrate a point, reference it with a link to the original.

The Fresh Content Crusade

The search engines are constantly looking for new content and now, with chronological searching, people are digging for results that happened in the last 24 hours, week, month, not just general results. They don't want to see results from 4 years ago, they want up to date information.

Adding new content regularly can help you to reach this audience hungry for the latest information. This is where using software like WordPress for your website management can give you an advantage. Because it was originally blogging software, new content can be added in with a date and time.

Note: I'm talking about installing WordPress on your own hosting as the CMS to run your website, not the free Wordpress.com blogging site.

Publishing to Other Sites

Obviously with so many types of publishing files that you can produce, you don't just need to put them on your own website. Give the content away in exchange for a link. For example a Microsoft Word DOC file can be uploaded to Docstoc.com.

You just need to take advantage of the free membership and join up. You can then share your DOC or DOCX files with the world. Better still, your member profile contains links back to you and you can also put a link in the DOC file.

MP3 files and podcasts can be added to iTunes in your own channel, which allows iTunes users to subscribe to your feed. Every time you add a new podcast, they will automatically download it or be notified of the new content.

Each time you share your files via another site, you build another link back to you and spread your web brand a little bit further.

There are literally thousands of these file sharing sites that you can use to promote your products and services by giving away free content.

Tip: A quick way to find more sites like Docstoc.com is to type "sites like docstoc" into Google. Seems obvious doesn't it! I found these straight away:

- DocShare.com
- doXtop.com
- Docuter.com
- Yudu.com
- Thinkfreedocs.com
- YouPublish.com

Aside from .doc files, there are loads of PowerPoint sites you can upload your .ppt files to like Slideshare.com. Every one will allow you to build a profile with a link back to your website plus the ones in the presentation.

Building Extra Websites

There is no rule which states that you can only have one website for your business. Sadly, I come across businesses every day that think this way. I think it harks back to the days when a good website was a huge investment in dollars.

These days, you buy new domains for under $15 and unlimited website hosting for $100 a year (that means you can put unlimited different websites on it).

With a little training, anyone can setup a basic website using WordPress in less than 30 minutes. Then all you need to do is upload a nice looking, free template and add your new content. It's really quite simple!

Don't get me wrong, I know that for non technical people, this can sound impossible but you can always hire someone via Elance to do it for you. Heck, on Fiverr.com, you can get it done for $5!

If you like to work with set branding, get your template adjusted to match then use it on all of your extra sites. That way, they all look similar but contain slightly different text and keyword focus.

Why not set up a series of keyword or product/service focused sites that link back to your main website? Believe me, if you buy some good, keyword containing domains, write some excellent content and do your SEO, you'll be surprised by the extra traffic you can get.

Building extra websites that link back to your main site allows you to do a couple of things:

- Focus the content on 1 topic or keyword.

- SEO the site to match that keyword.

- Go into more depth about your product or service.

- Provides a high quality link back to your main website.

- Casts a wider net developing more opportunities for people to find you in the search engines..

When ever I set up a new main business website, I often buy 5 more keyword focused domain names and set up mini sites on them. You only need a homepage, contact page, terms and conditions page, privacy page and an about us page to get started. It's quite simple to do and if you don't have time, you can always outsource it.

I've discovered that a good keyword rich domain with a compact WordPress site on it can often get high first page rankings in a matter of weeks. Granted, these aren't the most competitive terms but in many cases they bring 10-100 visitors a day. If your conversion ratio is good, they can be a great source of new business.

Tip: Learn how to install and setup a basic WordPress site yourself or train a staff member. With concentration, you can build about 10 or more of these mini sites a day after a couple of hours of practice. If you duplicate the first one and change the content around, you could potentially build more.

Watch my video on how to do this.

Link: *wordpress.mrwebmarketing.com*

Key Points to Action:

- Keep writing new content.

- Make sure you apply your SEO skills.

- Expand your products/services pages out to multiple pages.

- Setting up mini sites can bring more traffic for you.

- Learn to use and setup WordPress.

Steps to take today:

- Start writing a page about each of your products and services.

- Store the information in a Word doc.

Steps to take this month:

- Hire a content writer and start them writing regular content for your site.

- Build out your pages to about 300-500 words each.

- Review what you already have and improve it.

Case Study 5

Publishing

Success Certificates

Your website functions as your online business card, only instead of handing it out, people find it by searching for keywords and phrases in the search engines. If the keywords and phrases that people are searching for aren't found on your website, the search engines aren't going to display your site when those terms are searched for.

Why would you want to miss out on connecting with hundreds, thousands or even millions of people who are searching for products and services that you have to offer?

Good content is going to help get your website found in the search engines. It's also an element on your website that people are going to use to determine if they're going to return to your site in the future or not. Simply having content in place isn't good enough; you need to have valuable, informative and interesting content that people have a need for.

But why stop there? Unfortunately, most people only place attention on their website content and don't go any further. Your website isn't the only place that you should be publishing online if you want to see the maximum results. By not taking it a step further, you're missing out on these great benefits:

- Link building opportunities - when you publish content on other websites, there are times where you're going to be allowed to place a link or two in the content that points back to your website

- Brand exposure - every time you publish something online, whether it's a video, an article or any other type of publishing, you're exposing your name and your brand to the Internet community, which can help you become an authority figure in the niche that you're in

- Website traffic - when users view content that you publish on other websites and platforms, it helps generate traffic back to your website. Even if you can't place a link in the content, a user may be prompted to search for you, your website or your business

- Interacting - publishing online gives you a great opportunity to interact with current and potential customers. As this interaction takes place, you're able to build up trust and a good reputation with those who you're engaging

Publishing online sounds like a lot of work, how do I know it'll be effective?

Once you know the best places to go to publish content, you're going to get a system in place and it's not going to seem like a lot of work. Content publishing is also an area where a lot of businesses decide to outsource the work, which is especially beneficial when you want to make sure that it's being done correctly.

Still not convinced? Take a look at how one unique business has utilised online publishing to gain exposure, increase conversions and overtake their competition!

Introducing Success Certificates

Success Certificates is a unique company that provides online award certificates that you can download and print instantly.

Even though online award certificates isn't a niche that would seem very competitive, Success Certificates found that other companies who were offering the same services were beating them out in the search engine results.

What's special to note about this case is that this company offers completely free templates, but they were still losing out to their competition because their online marketing and search engine optimisation wasn't matching their competition.

Free Certificate Templates – Achievement Awards & Certificates!

This goes to show that just because you're offering a great product at a great price, doesn't mean that the business is going to be pouring in when selling online! You still need to go above and beyond in order to reach people and make the right connections.

The Plan

Success Certificates elected to start a major search engine optimisation campaign, with most of the focus being placed on content publishing. The focus was placed on those two areas with the specific goal of rising above their competition in the search engines so that they could start seeing the sales that they desired.

If they weren't going to be able to rise above their competition, there was a very small chance that they'd be as successful as they needed to be in selling their certificates online.

To help them meet their goals, the content and publishing that was implemented. They're:

- Improving existing content on their website, especially relating to product descriptions
- Finding keywords and phrases that would enable their website to be found above their competition in the search engines
- Writing and publishing press releases to help generate interest from the online community
- Utilising blogging to help bring in website traffic, build content and create interest
- Writing articles and publishing them to other websites and platforms
- Being consistent with publishing efforts

Success Certificates had very high goals to achieve through their content and publishing efforts; did they succeed?

The Results

They absolutely succeeded and they were able to start seeing all of the benefits from their efforts within a month! Success Certificates was able to rise above many of their competition, increase website traffic, build up their brand name, gain exposure and even increase links back to their website through their publishing efforts.

They now receive over 2000-8000 visitors a day from over 12,400 different keyword phrases and many more from linking sites who share their certificate templates with other users for free.

Considerations

When you have a website or an online business, it's hard enough to get your website to the first page of Google or the other search engines even if you don't have a lot of competition from other sites. When you do have a lot of competition, the challenge is even greater.

The websites that are currently listed above yours may already have good SEO in place. They may have also been in existence for many years- something Google takes into account when deciding where a website should be ranked.

Success Certificates had all of these challenges to overcome, plus more. Not only did they overcome them, they overcame them and came out on top! You don't need a special type of business in order to benefit from publishing content online.

Summary

Are you ready to grab the number one spot in Google for keywords and phrases that will drive traffic to your website? If the answer is yes, then online publishing is a must! You may have heard the phrase "content is king" once or twice before and you've heard it with good reason.

Writing good content comes with a whole bag of great benefits that can make the difference between seeing or not seeing online business success. It creates so many opportunities that it's impossible to list them all in one study.

What's even better is that publishing online is fun! It gives you and your business a creative outlet since you can inject videos, podcasts and other interactive ideas into your plan.

Link: *http://bit.ly/WufBX6*

Step 6

Video Everything And Share It Worldwide.

Step 6: Video Everything And Share It Worldwide.

We live a surprisingly video rich lifestyle. I guess we just don't think about it too often but we have the TV running even when we're not watching it, we video our events, and share links to funny videos. Video is all around us even when we don't think we watch that much of it.

Fact: Online video watching is taking people away from TV time. The number of people who are spending time watching video clips online rather than sitting in front of the TV is growing.

Of course, then there's the people like me who do both at once... madness! ☺ I think it's the result of my parents limiting my TV time when I was young or I may just be trying to consume every last bit of entertainment I can in my busy life. Who knows?

Who'd Have Thought It?

The key to this happening has been the rise in mobile broadband and fast home broadband connections. We can now download and watch video almost any where at any time.

In 2011, U.S. consumers spent an average of four hours and 20 minutes per month watching video on the web, a full hour and 10 minutes above what they spent in 2010

Unsurprisingly, age is the biggest factor in influencing video consumption habits. Adults ages 50 to 84 made up the largest chunk (25%) of traditional TV viewership, while adults ages 35 to 49 comprised the largest segment (27%) of the

Internet video audience. Meanwhile, 25 to 34-year-olds accounted for the highest percentage (30%) of mobile device video viewership.

Now that you know the "facts", what are you doing in the online video arena?

Why Bother Going to all the Trouble of Recording Videos?

If you haven't looked lately, the search engines are now showing video listings in their search results. In many cases they rank on the first page for searches that return millions of matching pages. Submitting a keyword titled video has the potential to jump to the top in days, not months.

Some businesses have discovered this and use this as their only means of promotion online. And, in some cases, their work has been handsomely rewarded in visitors to their websites or social media profiles.

If you're just starting out though, videos of testimonials, product demonstrations, etc make excellent additions to your website as they build familiarity and trust for you.

Starting Down the Video Road.

Before you jump up, grab the video camera and start shooting, you should lay out a plan on what you're hoping to achieve with these videos. Of course you can just shoot random footage and upload it but thinking back to Chapter 1, wouldn't it make more sense to produce targeted search engine content?

Don't try to shoot a feature length film. Aim at making your videos between 30sec and 2 minutes long.

I've always found that the most natural place for businesses looking to start shooting short videos is by answering a list of commonly asked questions. In most cases, they already have a FAQ page on their website with these already written.

Only choose the ones that lend themselves to an explanation. Videos where you justify your prices seem to be less education and effective which normally doesn't help sell you or your products to the people watching.

Take the most asked question first, write down 5 short points that answer it or if you like, write out what you are going to say. As you get more comfortable in front of a camera, you'll find it easier to work from a list of points. Practice your answer a couple of times until you feel comfortable and natural with it.

Like any advertising, I'd suggest that you introduce yourself, answer your question then direct people to your website or phone.

You can see an example of a short answer video here:

Link: *youtube.com/mrwebmarketing*

Brad's Video Formula that Never Fails

I use a simple formula. It goes something like this. I introduce myself. I talk about what I want to talk about and then I reintroduce myself. I'll say:

> "Hi, I'm **Brad Hauck**, the Online Productivity Expert. I help people get faster online results in less time. Today I wanted to talk to you about..."

==Content of video==

I hope you've learned something. I'm Brad Hauck from the Australian Institute of Internet Marketing if you'd like to learn more about what we do and how we can help you please call us on 1300 793 700 or go to www.AIIMtraining.com.au "

Introduce myself, deliver my content, reintroduce myself...

Editing Your Videos

You don't need high end video editing equipment to tidy up your videos. Most people find the free iMovie (Mac) or Windows Movie Maker (Win) do a fantastic job of allowing you to remove the pause at the start and end of your videos, add transitions, titles and overlays and export to a movie file. Most software now also has the ability to upload directly to YouTube and other sites at the click of your mouse.

Take 2 minutes to add your branding to every video you shoot. Make sure you do because if someone embeds your video, you want them to show your link. You should ensure that they can't get rid of it by placing it over the whole video.

YouTube Records Live!

Thanks to Google, if you have a webcam built into or connected to your computer, you can record a video directly to the YouTube website.

They have also included a new tool called the Video Editor which allows you to edit your own uploaded clips to produce an entirely new video. With the Video Editor, you can:

- Combine multiple videos to create a new longer video.

- Trim your uploads to custom size.
- Add a soundtrack from the library of approved tracks.
- Customise videos with special tools and effects.

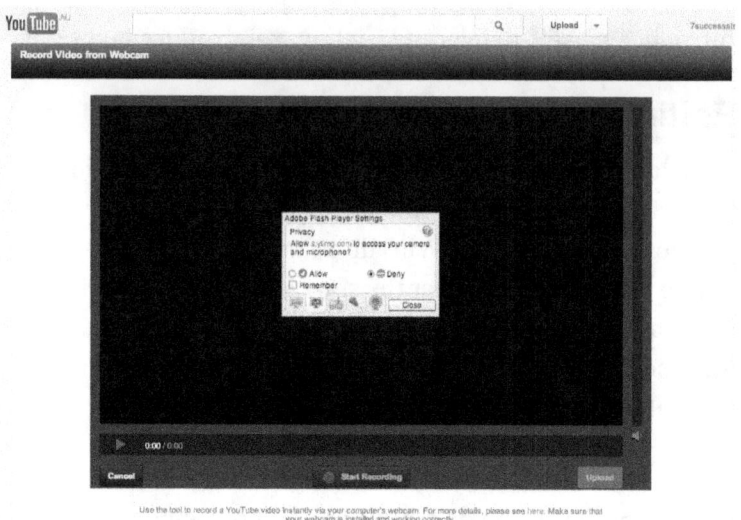

Using these tools, you can put together clips to create new videos online from anywhere in the world and publish the new video to YouTube with one click.

So why would you bother with this when you have built in software? It's pretty simple... convenience! From anywhere in the world you can login, shoot a quick video that gets your message out to the people you want to reach.

Pro v Homemade

Your videos don't need to be "high end" when you're updating people on new products and services. Quite the opposite. People seem to like the raw video more sometimes.

Don't get me wrong, there's a place for professional video and that's where you're trying to make a great first impression but testimonials, updates and tips are more believable when a bit amateurish.

If you're going to record a professional video, make sure you script what you're going to say, think about your message and practice before you start.

Having a good script and knowing it makes you sound confident and professional. I recommend that you always run through what you're going to say out loud a few times before you press the record button.

There's an advantage to shooting short videos, not too much to remember ☺

Where Do You Put Your Videos?

Obviously, YouTube is the big daddy of video sharing. With Google owning the site, you can be assured that you'll get maximum exposure from the search engines.

One of the best features of using YouTube and other video sharing sites is that you don't have to host the video yourself. You just upload it to them then copy and paste a bit of code into your website to display the video for your readers.

YouTube will adjust the video feed automatically so your watchers see the best quality feed possible for their internet connection speed.

Getting Your Videos to Rank

Sometimes shooting video and adding it to video sharing sites is just about getting a link back to your main site but why not take advantage of the possible rankings and optimise it?

When you upload a video to video sharing sites, they ask you to fill out a title, description and category information. It's in these fields that you can slip in your link.

Start your title with your keywords making sure that it sounds interesting to someone who sees it. Use the keywords that you're trying to rank for because in Google's search results we see news, images, videos and more all mixed together.

Insert your URL like this, *http://www.mrwebmarketing.com* as the first thing in your description field. Follow this with a normal description that fully describes the video, its content and who recorded it.

You can often fit quite a lot of information into this field. Most people stop at one sentence so try writing a couple of paragraphs and see what happens. It can often make a big difference to where you rank within the video sharing site as well as the search engines.

One technique that seems to work well is to add a full transcription of what you have said in your video into the description box. Not only is it keyword focused text, it helps Google define what to rank your video for as they can't yet understand all of what you say.

Don't Stop at YouTube

There are literally hundreds of video sharing sites that you can upload your video to. From Veoh to Daily Motion, these sites operate in a similar way to YouTube.

T

he more places you upload your video to, the more chances of it showing up in the search results. I've found that Daily Motion tends to rank very well. Take the time to SEO your upload and link them back to your website.

There are some sites like these at *videosharing.mrwebmarketing.com* that allow you to upload once then they share it to your profiles on a range of video sharing sites for you. Tools like these speed up your work and save you time.

Remember that you can also strip the audio from your video and upload that to sites that share MP3 files. If you're doing training videos, why not upload them to iTunes as a podcast?

Do it Regularly

Most businesses start out with good intentions to shoot video every week. Having tried to do this myself, you soon find that life gets in the way. You DO need to upload regular videos just like doing regular link building is necessary for fast online success.

I suggest you plan and record 10-20 videos at once. Being only 30 seconds to 2 minutes long, it should only take you a couple of hours. You can then hire someone, if necessary to edit them (what I call top & tailing them) for you. It's cheaper if they do it all in one go.

I recommend ringing a specialist like Scott Bowerman at Upload Media.

Link: *www.UploadMedia.com.au*

Key Points to Action:

- Check to see what recording equipment you already have.

- Find out what editing software you have installed.

- Create accounts on a range of video sharing sites.

- Make a list of video titles to shoot.

- Write some scripts & practice.

- Record, edit and upload your videos

- Do the SEO on each video and link to your website.

- Do it regularly.

Steps to take today:

- Make a list of 10 videos you could record easily.

- Find someone to record them for you.

Steps to take this month:

- Call Upload Media about their services.

- Record your first video and upload.

- Track to see if it ranks.

- Plan your video series.

Case Study 6

Video

BlendTec

It's no secret that online video marketing can take a person or a business from a nobody to a somebody literally overnight. You also don't need to look very far before seeing the true power of video marketing. Justin Bieber anyone?

Sure, he's a celebrity in the U.S., but what many don't realise is that he gained his fame by posting videos of his music talents on YouTube. His videos were viewed by a person who ended up becoming his manager, who then made the appropriate connections in the music industry.

But what does Justin Bieber have to do with using video marketing for businesses? He's one of the most famous examples of how online videos can be used for business success. He wasn't selling a product or service on YouTube, but what he was selling was his voice, a voice that's now turned into a multi-million dollar singing career.

Let's deal with the obvious, not everyone is Justin Bieber, but you don't have to be in order to see astronomical results from video marketing. You don't even need to have an exciting product or service! To further prove this point, think about the exact opposite of Justin Bieber.

Instead of a famous celebrity with a now massive following, think about a household item that everyone has but that's more than likely stuffed in a cabinet somewhere collecting dust. This household item has two main functions most of the time and it typically only comes out to play when you want to sip on frozen drink or you have a family barbeque.

The bland and boring household item being referred to is the blender. You can use it to crush ice, you can use it to make drinks and you can also use it if for one reason or another, you're restricted to a liquid diet. It's not Justin Bieber, but it has its uses! But can you video market with it online? Sure you can and in this case study, you're going to see how one company saw online marketing success using videos and the blenders that they sell.

Who wants to watch a YouTube video about blenders? You'd be greatly surprised. So if you think that the products or services that you offer are too boring for videos, this case will definitely make you think again!

Introducing BlendTec

If you haven't guessed by now, BlendTec makes blenders. They're a U.S. based company but in this case it doesn't matter where they're from. You could be located in Australia, the U.S. or the backwoods of Siberia and it'd still be difficult to market blenders online! How in the world do you market blenders?

Most people would agree that a blender is not a product that they spend too much time thinking about. It serves a general purpose and while some may have a few more nifty features than others, they're essentially all the same. Internet users also don't generally spend a great deal of time being entertained by blender information when they're browsing online.

Not only are blenders boring, but there's so many of them! It's actually a very over-saturated and competitive business where it's hard to make one blender stand out above the rest. The owner of BlendTec knew that he needed a way to reach consumers that were going to get their attention and not bore them to death.

In the blender industry, word of mouth marketing isn't even applicable...have you ever heard someone recommend a blender or ask for a recommendation of one? Probably not!

The Plan

BlendTec knew that they needed to do something beyond the traditional means of advertising. Who wants to see a television or newspaper ad for blenders? That type of marketing just doesn't work- not to mention, it's incredibly expensive!

BlendTec turned to the Internet and to video marketing to help reach their customer base. The plan was to create a series of YouTube videos that would catch consumer attention and be interesting at the same time- a difficult challenge in the blender world, but the plan was genius!

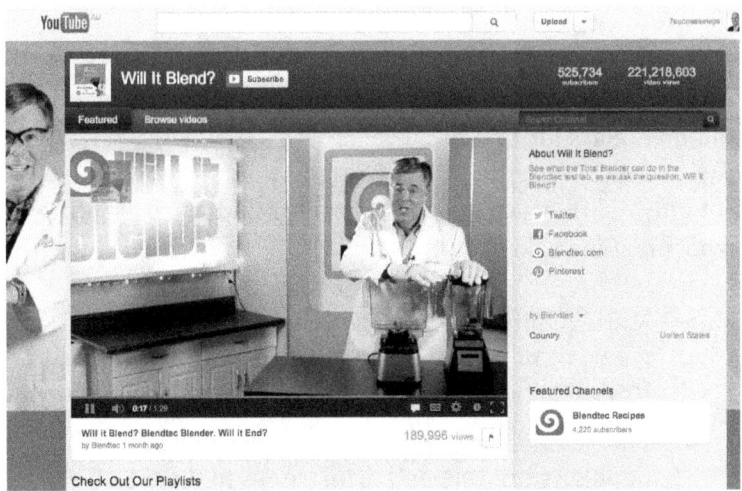

BlendTec developed a series of YouTube videos called "Will It Blend?" From the title, the plot of the videos shouldn't be too hard for you to figure out. They took a boring household appliance and developed videos that were interesting and fun to watch. Will it blend? People wanted to know and they watched!

The Results

Not only did the video marketing campaign work, but it went viral! How viral? Try millions of unique views- per video! Not just millions of views for all of their videos combined, but each video that they have posted (and there's been many) have averaged 2 to 3 million unique views, with some of them reaching over 10 million views! Have you ever had over 10 million people view your product?

No one wants to sit there and watch someone blend the usual suspects- so how about an iPhone, golf balls or even skis? Now that's something people will watch! Stepping aside from the astronomical amount of video views, let's talk profit.

During the year after their video marketing campaign was launched, the company was projected to make well over 50 million dollars for that fiscal year!

Not only did they achieve higher profits and more brand exposure, they also gained:

- More quality backlinks to their website- as video views went up and the videos went viral, websites from around the globe were linking to the company

- The blenders are now used by some of the most popular smoothie and drink shops in the U.S.

- An increase in website visitors

- A massive social media following

People didn't know BlendTec before but they know BlendTec now! Their video marketing campaign is one of the most popular viral marketing video series to ever be released.

Considerations

How much does something like this cost? BlendTec recorded their videos with a standard HD camera, which can typically be picked up for a few hundred dollars or less. On top of that, many digital cameras are now coming equipped with HD recording equipment built in, so you may even already have what you need to start shooting!

YouTube and other video platforms on the Internet are also free to post to. Most people and businesses can easily put together a video or a set of videos with very little money- all you really need is a creative idea and the ambition to make it work!

When it comes down to it, most businesses offer products or services that people need- not luxury items that are exciting and that people want. This case study goes to show that even if your business involves very boring products or services, you can still find a way to market online and reach a ton of people in a very short period of time.

It doesn't have to be a blender; it can be a book, a new style of shoes, a new website application or in the case of Chuck Testa, a taxidermy business! If your voice or other talent is what you want to sell, you already know that it's possible with posting videos online.

Summary

Using videos to market your products or services online is

cost effective, easy to do and it works! The above example is just one out of many success stories that could've been used to showcase just how powerful using videos is.

Why does it work? People are simply spending more time online these days and away from their televisions. Rather than spend an enormous amount of money on an advertising outlet that people aren't spending a lot of time on anymore, why not save the money and go to where the consumers are? Another reason why it works is because it's fun, engaging and interactive.

It lets people see your company in a different light. They can find out all of the information that you want them to know, while entertaining those who are viewing the videos at the same time. People are done with boring advertising- they want to be engaged.

Finally, videos also help show that you care about your company and the products or services that you have to offer. If you're going to take the time out to make a video or a series of video to reach people, then it tells people that you're serious about connecting with people.

To some companies that offer them, a blender is a hopeless household good to market- but to BlendTec, it's not just any household good, it's their business and they cared enough to make their business grow through video marketing.

Link: *http://bit.ly/T84raM*

Step 7

Plan to Succeed Quickly & Efficiently

Step 7: Plan to Succeed Quickly & Efficiently

The fact of the matter is that if you don't plan to succeed online you go around and around in circles never completing any of the 7 steps successfully.

Why? Because there's always something new to learn. It seems that *bright shiny object syndrome* rules the online marketing community.

Sadly, this is a formula for failure if you're running a "real business". Most of these schemes and tricks work for a very short time and the people who sell them to you plan for their websites to have a very limited lifespan. That's generally unacceptable for most businesses.

Many people approach online marketing in a haphazard sort of way. They will look at the steps of this book, or any system, and try to complete them one by one without first putting together a plan.

If you really want success online, you need to have a strict plan and follow it from week to week so that you know what you are going to do before each day starts.

Writing a Publishing Plan

A publishing plan is an absolutely essential part of success online. The reason for this is that most people sit down at the computer and think to themselves, "What am I going to write today?"

Anyone who has had anything to do with the publishing industry understands that you need a publishing plan to follow each month. For example, each year just before summer, you'll find that sports and men's magazines always cover stories about losing weight and getting fit.

They don't need to think about what they are going to write because in January they start collecting ideas and articles to put into that September edition.

What are you doing to make sure that your business flows comfortably from month to month?

Have you taken the time to put together a plan or at least a list of themes which you going to cover over the next 12 months? If not, now is the time to start the process. It's never too late to get a plan in place.

In this chapter, I'm going to take you through the process that I use to write a powerful online marketing plan to help business succeed online. This is a fairly basic tool but it will set you apart from most of your competitors and put you in the position whereby you don't need to worry about what you're going to do online, you'll already know when you sit down.

If you want a publishing plan but don't have time to do one, my team can put one together for you. Just contact us.

It's Too Much Trouble

Why bother putting together a publishing plan when you already know what your business is all about and what you do for people? It's really quite simple. Having this plan means that you can bring in outside help if you need to. You can outsource or you can hire someone and hand them the plan to follow.

This not only leverages your time, which improves your efficiency and saves time, but it insures that you keep regular content creation happening so that your business keeps people who follow your updates interested but also makes the search engines happy.

Most businesses I've been to, never think past what they're going to write today let alone planning what to write tomorrow or next month.

Monthly plan

Let's begin the planning process with a monthly plan. Using the table below, layout what topic you're going to cover over the next 12 months.

The key to making a publishing plan work for you, not against you, is to ensure that the topics work well with the keywords that you have chosen for your website SEO.

For example, if your chosen keywords are *car washing*, and your whole business is about *car washing*, then each month of your plan should be built around this topic e.g.

- January: hand car washing
- February: Prestige car washing
- March: car washing cleaning products
- April: automatic car washing

You can see from the four month example above that every month we're still talking about car washing but we discuss a different aspect of car washing.

In January, we'll talk always about hand car washing and the advantages of having your car hand washed.

In February, because we want to get more prestige cars, we going to talk about getting prestige cars washed and how getting a hand wash is definitely better than putting their car through an automatic washing.

In March we're going to talk about all different car washing cleaning products and we'll talk about how the quality of the products we use as they're so much better than the cheap brands.

In April we going to talk about automatic car washing and are going to focus on the damage and the negative aspects of using automatic car washing.

Remember you're not just going to write articles. You going to use all of the 6 steps that we covered so far. You're going to use video, articles, press releases, social media, photos, etc.

Monthly Publishing Topics

January	
February	
March	
April	
May	
June	
July	
August	
September	
October	
November	
December	

Stop now and complete the table above on a page in your notebook or right here if you wish!

If you don't have a notebook, you should have one. It's the perfect place to store ideas and information over time. I have one that I've had for about four years and I just keep adding ideas to it as I think of them. I can then review them when I run out of things to do ☺

Once you've completed your plan you can then transfer it to your calendar so that on the first of each month it comes up with what your publishing angle is going to be for that month. If you have a wall calendar, you can put it there too so that everybody in the office can see what they'll be writing or talking about in that month.

Remember, this is the topic of the month, you don't stray from the topic and you keep focused on it *in all aspects of your business communications.*

Weekly plan

The weekly plan is where you lay out what you're going to talk about or write about during the week in more specific words.

This is where you can apply some of those keyword search tools to find long-tail phrases. You can use these to form the basis of posts, articles, status updates, vidos, etc. The list below comes from the bottom of a Google search page where it shows other popular searches:

- washing car with hand soap
- hand washing your car
- what to use when hand washing your car
- how to properly hand wash a car
- what do you wash your car with

- car hand wash steps
- how to hand wash a car fast
- wash new car by hand

As you can see from this list, it would be quite easy to turn each one into a statement or question to write about in your blog post or article. If you were to take this list and use one each day, you would have more than a week planned. Then you only need to find a few more to fill in the rest of the month.

Whether you write these out into a specific table, or you just build a list like the one above and tick them off as you work your way through the month, is up to you.

Personally, I would just leave them as a big list and cross them off as I work through the month. Remember, the more research you do now, the less you have to sit down and do at the start of each month.

It's better to take a day at the start of the year to plan this out than to try to come up with a list of titles/topics every month. If you try to leave it until the start of the month, I'll lay odds on that you won't get around to it.

You're just too busy to spend that much time each month with your hectic schedule.

On the next page, take the time to lay out a weekly publishing plan and think about what you're trying to achieve.

Weekly Publishing Plan

Sunday	
Monday	
Tuesday	
Wednesday	
Thursday	
Friday	
Saturday	

Stop now and complete the table above on a page in your notebook or right here if you wish!

Daily plan

Your daily plan is more about what you going to do rather than what you're going to talk about.

It's about whether you're going to write a blog post on Monday and then follow it with a series of social media status updates more so than the topic you're writing about.

Because we have so much to do, but we generally have a small amount of time in which to do it, having a plan that you can follow on a daily basis that's repeated from week to week, month to month, will make your life much easier.

It will also allow you to outsource content creation and posting update etc to someone else.

I'm all for quality content, but I also believe that to get the best results you need to leverage yourself. The only way to do that is by using other people's skills.

Your daily plan should reflect what audience you're trying to reach. If you're using social media and your audience is in LinkedIn, and then you should list more work on that platform rather than Facebook.

If you look at the example plan below, you'll see tasks like blogging, social updates, audio recordings, adding to content sharing sites and more. Each time you complete a task, you make another link back to you for readers to follow.

Example Plan

Monday	Blog post, tweet, LinkedIn
Tuesday	Record audio of post content, share iTunes, all SM
Wednesday	Video self speaking post content, share on YouTube, add to website
Thursday	2nd Post of week, Share to all SM
Friday	Put post content into article and add to article sites, doc sharing sites
Saturday	Add MP3 to audio sharing sites
Sunday	Rest ;-)

Too Complicated?

This plan may seem a little complicated at first to you but it does give an indication of how you can lay things out in a pattern that can be repeated. Depending on your level of technical expertise, converting a article to audio may seem a little difficult at first. But, if you download a program like Audacity, you'll find it's relatively simple and instructions can be found online.

To start with, why not sit down and write out a basic plan that you feel you can fulfill each week. As you progress, you can add in new steps or outsource them to others.

Take 5 minutes now and write.

Some Free Help: My 21 Day Kickstarter

If you go to 21days.Mrwebmarketing.com and sign up, I'll send you 21 daily task to do that will kick start your Internet marketing very quickly and will help you to learn a successful repeatable process. By the end of 21 days, you'll have a process that you can repeat over and over successfully.

What makes this short-course so powerful, is that I only set you one simple task at a time to complete for that day. Most of the tasks can be completed within 10 to 15 minutes. A couple of tasks might take a bit longer, but you'll be able to use the information you collect time and time again.

You'll also be able to apply the steps and skills that you have learnt in this book.

Link: *21days.mrwebmarketing.com*

Compiling Your Final Plan

It's all very well to sit there and read this book, but what you really need to do is take action if you're going to see any results. If you follow the seven steps in this book and you continue to repeat what you have learnt, month after month, you will see a massive change in your results.

As I said very early on in the steps, more than 90% of your competition will probably never get past Step 2 and if they do they will only complete a couple of the techniques you now know. For example, they may go ahead and shoot five YouTube videos and upload them but they won't share them to other sites and they'll probably never shoot another YouTube video again.

Review what you've written as you've read through Step 7 and make it a part of your routine. Please implement it so that you can see how it can grow your online business results.

Key Points to Action:

- Plan to succeed.

- You need a publishing plan.

- Knowing what you're going to write about saves time and frustration in the long term.

- A plan makes it easier to outsource work too.

Steps to take today:

- Make a list of keyword related topics for your business.

- Fill in the 12 month topic table.

Steps to take this month:

- Complete all of the plans.

- Do keyword research for article titles

- Start implementing your plan.

- Keep it up!

The Secret

The Key Ingredient of Online Success

So what is the Secret to Success Online?

Ok, so this is my opinion and others may have other ideas but this is what I think, based upon over 20 years online.

It's funny, but many people think there is a silver bullet to success online. Thanks to the Internet gurus out there that spruke their hype from stages, many people are being led to believe that there some is some secret that you can buy.

There isn't.

The truth behind success online is no different from the truth behind success in business.

This secret is consistent action combined with positive interaction with your customers on an ongoing basis.

That means you need to write content regularly, you need to use your social media, you need to produce videos on a regular basis, answer your emails, call your clients and you need to repeat the process week after week, month after month, year after year if you want to see ongoing sales and profit growth.

If you stop this process, you'll hold your positions and your customers for a time but your results will start to erode day by day eventually resulting in a fall in rankings and drop in traffic which will massively affect the bottom line.

Why? Because your competitors are working against you and they want nothing more than your top rankings and your clients.

Plan to Succeed

So how do you achieve this on an ongoing basis? You plan to succeed.

In step seven we looked at compiling a plan of what to do on a monthly basis. It is absolutely essential that you do this and follow it. If you don't have time to follow it, then you need to learn how to outsource these tasks to someone else, somewhere else in the world.

You may not find someone straightaway who can do this successfully to the standard that you expect, but after trialing a couple of people, I have no doubt that you will find someone to help you.

The best thing about putting a plan into place is that you can realistically repeat your topics every single year. That means that the topics you talk about on a monthly basis can be repeated just with new articles and new information.

Why? Because the content you're creating is designed to attract search engine attention and the searches of users who are looking for your products and services. People are likely to be looking for the same keywords over many years because their needs tend to be the same.

Educating Yourself or Your Staff

Self education and the training of your staff is essential to ongoing success if you're not going to outsource your work to someone else.

In this book, I have quickly covered the basics of what you need to know but the specific skills that you need to learn to apply take a little bit longer to cover.

To help you succeed in this area, I have produced a course that will teach you all the skills that you need to know to get your online marketing started.

At the Australian Institute of Internet marketing (www.AIIMtraining.com.au), we have a range of courses including a diploma and certificate course in which you can learn how to market online from me.

I recommend you look at the "Supercharge Your Online Marketing" course as it covers nine essential units which will help you succeed online. Each unit comes with over two hours of live video training delivered in HD video. All the training is me and you'll feel as if you're in the classroom plus you also get access to the content to read and learn from.

Better still, it's tax deductible!

Link:

- *www.aiimtraining.com.au*
- *supercharge.mrwebmarketing.com*

Things Change

Online, things do change over time. Even though in this book, I've focused on things that have been consistently working since 1996, there have been new things that have come and gone.

Keep reading, watching, testing and trialing and learn what works for your market.

See you in my next book!

Brad Hauck ☺

Kick Start Your Online Marketing in 21 Days!

Every day for 21 days, I will email you a business driving, quick and easy task that will get your online marketing humming...

Think of it as positive reinforcement of what you have learnt in this book. Each task has a short video showing you what you need to do and how to do it.

- Simple to do
- Once a day
- Gets things moving
- Guaranteed to work

As a free gift to you for reading my book, I'd like to give this course to you. It's free to sign up now! All you need to do is go to the web page below and start:

http://21days.mrwebmarketing.com

FREE GIFT!